PostgreSQL Configuration

Best Practices for Performance and Security

Baji Shaik

Apress®

PostgreSQL Configuration

Baji Shaik
Hyderabad, Andhra Pradesh, India

ISBN-13 (pbk): 978-1-4842-5662-6   ISBN-13 (electronic): 978-1-4842-5663-3
https://doi.org/10.1007/978-1-4842-5663-3

Managing Director, Apress Media LLC: Welmoed Spahr
Acquisitions Editor: Nikhil Karkal
Development Editor: Matthew Moodie
Coordinating Editor: Divya Modi

Cover designed by eStudioCalamar

Cover image designed by Freepik (www.freepik.com)

Distributed to the book trade worldwide by Springer Science+Business Media New York, 1 New York Plaza, New York, NY 10004. Phone 1-800-SPRINGER, fax (201) 348-4505, e-mail orders-ny@springer-sbm.com, or visit www.springeronline.com. Apress Media, LLC is a California LLC and the sole member (owner) is Springer Science + Business Media Finance Inc (SSBM Finance Inc). SSBM Finance Inc is a **Delaware** corporation.

For information on translations, please e-mail rights@apress.com, or visit www.apress.com/rights-permissions.

Apress titles may be purchased in bulk for academic, corporate, or promotional use. eBook versions and licenses are also available for most titles. For more information, reference our Print and eBook Bulk Sales web page at www.apress.com/bulk-sales.

Any source code or other supplementary material referenced by the author in this book is available to readers on GitHub via the book's product page, located at www.apress.com/978-1-4842-5662-6. For more detailed information, please visit http://www.apress.com/source-code.

Printed on acid-free paper

To Afrah Razzak, my wife, for her support and patience during long nights of writing.

Table of Contents

About the Author

Baji Shaik is a database administrator and developer. He was introduced to databases in 2011 and over the years has worked with Oracle, PostgreSQL, Postgres Advance Server, RedShift, and Greenplum. He has a wide range of expertise and experience in SQL/NoSQL databases such as Cassandra and DynamoDB. He is a database migration expert and has developed many successful database solutions addressing challenging business requirements for moving databases from on-premises to AWS Cloud using multiple AWS services. Baji has organized a number of PostgreSQL meet-ups and maintains his own technical blog, where he likes to share his knowledge with the community. He co-authored *Beginning PostgreSQL on the Cloud,* released in March 2018.

About the Technical Reviewer

 **Jobin Augustine** is a PostgreSQL expert and open source advocate and has more than 18 years of working experience as a consultant, architect, administrator, writer, and trainer in PostgreSQL, Oracle, and other database technologies. He has always been an active participant in the open source communities, and his main focus area is database performance and optimization. He is a regular face in many of the PostgreSQL conferences. He is a contributor to various open source projects, is an active blogger, and loves to code in C++ and Python. Jobin holds a Masters in Computer Applications and joined Percona in 2018 as a Senior Support Engineer. Prior to joining Percona, he worked at OpenSCG for 2 years as an Architect and was part of the BigSQL core team, a complete PostgreSQL distribution offering. Previous to his work at OpenScg, Jobin worked at Dell as a Database Senior Advisor for 10 years and 5 years with TCS/CMC.

Acknowledgments

I have many people to thank, as without them, this book would not have been possible. Thanks to Apress Media for believing in this book and providing me this opportunity. Thanks to Nikhil Karkal and Divya Modi for working with me and giving me extended time in busy schedules. Thanks to my Guru, Dinesh Kumar. Thanks to Matthew Moodie, Jobin Augustine and Will McGugan for reviewing the book. And thanks to my lovely wife Afrah Razzak for all the support during writing - it was all OUR time that I put in this book writing. And thanks to my loving parents—Lalu Saheb Shaik and Nasar Bee—because of them, I am who I am today.

Introduction

As PostgreSQL is one of most advanced open-source databases in the world, there are lot of sources available for major activities like installation, configuration, monitoring, high availability, maintenance, and security. However, it is important to know what information we require to build a strategy for any of these activities.

This book will walk you through how to get the information that you need and how to build strategies based on the information available. You will first get an overview of installation procedures and some recommendations and post-installation procedures to avoid performance issues in future. And then it will talk about configuring the database in-terms of parameters as basic configuration is tuned for compatibility rather than performance. Security of a database is always one of the major concerns so this book will focus on ways of securing PostgreSQL databases. This book will also explain logging and monitoring of the database which help in troubleshooting issues and prevent the issues in future.

Building backup/restore strategies is based on many factors. This book will cover approaches to backup and restore a database based on which you can choose the right one for your environment. One of the key things that we should take care while working with PostgreSQL is maintenance. This book will help you to understand the maintenance activities of PostgreSQL and how to execute them to get a good performance.

Designing High Availability is always tough as it may need some other opensource or enterprise tools to be involved. This book will go through all high availability procedures available in PostgreSQL and some HA designs that you can consider. If you have application with large number of users, connection overhead can become a big problem which can be overcome using Connection Poolers. This book will cover the available connection poolers and challenges. And finally, this book will show you some basic errors while working with PostgreSQL and their causes and resolutions. It helps if you are new to PostgreSQL.

CHAPTER 1

Best Ways to Install PostgreSQL

This chapter covers the best ways to install PostgreSQL. It answers the following questions:

1. What information do you need to install PostgreSQL on a server?

2. What prerequisites should you follow?

3. What are the best ways to install PostgreSQL?

4. What are the post-installation steps that make your life easier?

5. How do you troubleshoot installation issues?

6. How do you tune operating system (OS) parameters to avoid issues in the future?

PostgreSQL is one of the most advanced open source databases in the world. If anyone wants to migrate from an enterprise database to an open source database to save some money, or for better security by use of fully auditable source code or custom development, PostgreSQL is one of the best databases to consider. It has a rich feature set and is famous for constant major releases. Its huge community ensures the stability of

© Baji Shaik 2020
B. Shaik, *PostgreSQL Configuration*, https://doi.org/10.1007/978-1-4842-5663-3_1

the database by continuously fixing bugs and adding new development features, including a high percentage of ANSI SQL compliance with which it competes with other major enterprise databases in the market.

Before you can use PostgreSQL, you need to install it. As it is open source, there are multiple ways to install it. It depends on the environment in which you are going to install and the PostgreSQL distribution you install. Not all environments are user friendly to follow the same installation procedure. So, it is very important to get as much information as you can before you install it.

Sometimes, customers might not be able to provide all the details needed for installation. So, as an admin, you need to explicitly ask for the information required. It is always recommended to have a conversation with your customer about this. To ensure an effective conversation about installation, it is important to know what information you need and why you need it.

Information Needed for Installation

In this section, we are going to cover answers to the question: What information do we need to have for installing PostgreSQL on a server?

Here are a few questions through which you will get the details to install PostgreSQL.

Note   Every question has a specific purpose added to it, which helps in the conversation with the customer and to proceed further.

Q1.   What is the operating system? What is the architecture of the OS (32/64 bit)?

Purpose: This is a basic question that you should ask. Installation procedures vary from one OS to another. So, it is important to know which OS you are going to install. It helps you in planning the installation, which we are going to talk about in later sections of the chapter.

Q2.   What are the machine specifications (RAM, CPU)?

Purpose: PostgreSQL uses some shared memory (based on its configuration) while it is up and running. So, based on the server's memory, you should plan to set shared memory of the OS. It can be set through some kernel parameters, which will be covered later in this chapter.

Q3.   What is the current size and expected growth of the application?

Purpose: How much storage should be allocated to PostgreSQL depends on the current data size and expected growth of data. In general, companies plan storage based on growth in the future. It is recommended to plan by keeping the next 3 to 5 years of growth in mind.

Q4.   What is the type of storage?

Purpose: Different storages have different behavior with PostgreSQL. So, it is recommended to know what kind of storage—like magnetic disks, SSD (Solid State Drive), NVMe (Non-Volatile Memory express),

SAN (Storage Area Network), LVM (Logical Volume Management), or cloud storage like EBS (Elastic Block Store)—that the customer wants to use.

Q5.   What filesystem is being used by the server?

Purpose: One of the key factors that affect PostgreSQL performance is the filesystem type. You should know what filesystem is currently on the server and what recommendations you can give to get the best performance. As it varies from application to application and environment to environment (basically, it depends on workload types), you should really benchmark your performance for the filesystems available and decide which is the best suited for your application. However, there are some general recommendations of filesystem types for PostgreSQL, which we will talk about in the "General Recommendations for PostgreSQL Disk/Storage" section.

Q6.   How many mount points?

Purpose: This question helps you to know about current mount points on the server. PostgreSQL is designed to write into multiple files when something is selected/inserted/updated/deleted in the database. So, disk IO becomes a bottleneck most of the time. If you can plan to add mount points as needed, it would distribute the IO across mount points so that IO bottlenecks can be avoided, which would reduce much IO consumption on the server. We discuss what files get written and how to plan for multiple mount points in a later section of the chapter.

Q7. Is public Internet accessible from the server?

Purpose: Depending on the installation you choose, it is necessary to know if the server can access the public Internet or not. This may affect the way you install PostgreSQL software and do future maintenance, including upgrades. If the server cannot connect to the public Internet, you need to download the required software packages on a server that has Internet access and copy those software packages to a production server through a private network or whatever way possible for the customer.

To plan for the right installation procedure, you need to know answers to the preceding questions.

Types of Installations

Let us talk about types of installations before we plan for the installation. You can install PostgreSQL in four ways.

- Source installation

- Binary installation

- RPM installation

- One-click installer

As PostgreSQL is open source, the source code is available on the PostgreSQL web site (`postgresql.org`). We are going to cover each installation method in detail as follows.

Source Installation

Source install is nothing but compiling the source code of PostgreSQL. You need not be a coding expert to compile the source code. However, you need to understand each step of the installation so that you can troubleshoot installation issues.

The following are the high-level steps that you can take to install from source.

Note   PostgreSQL Version 11.4 is used in the following example. Similar steps work for other versions also.

---

1. You can download the source from the PostgreSQL official web site (postgresql.org).

    To download from browser:

    ```
    https://ftp.postgresql.org/pub/source/v11.4/postgresql--
    11.4.tar.bz2
    ```

    On Linux:

    ```
    wget https://ftp.postgresql.org/pub/source/v11.4/
    postgresql-11.4.tar.bz2
    ```

    On Mac:

    ```
    curl -O https://ftp.postgresql.org/pub/source/v11.4/
    postgresql-11.4.tar.bz2
    ```

2. Unpack the downloaded file as follows:

    ```
    tar -xf postgresql-11.4.tar.bz2
    All the source files will be unpacked into a directory
    postgresql-11.4
    ```

3. Go inside the directory created in step 2 and run the configure command as follows:

```
cd postgresql-11.4
./configure
```

The default installation directory for final PostgreSQL binaries is /usr/local/pgsql. If you want to install it in a different location, then a prefix option can be used for the configure command as follows.

```
./configure --prefix=/location/to/install/
```

configure command basically looks at your machine for dependency libraries necessary for PostgreSQL. It reports if your machine is missing any. You can install missing libraries first and then rerun the configure command. So basically, you prepare your machine for compiling the PostgreSQL source code at this stage. If you are not able to capture configure information while it is running or the terminal is closed after configure command fails, it creates a config.log in the same location from where you are running the configure command. Using this log, you will see configure command output.

If your application is going to be designed to use languages like Perl, Python, Tcl, etc. at the database side, then you need to opt for corresponding language packages locations using the following parameters:

```
--with-perl
--with-python
--with-tcl
```

In the same way, if you want to use OpenSSL, provide OpenSSL libs using the following parameter:

```
--with-openssl
```

There are multiple options available based on the requirement. You can get help for configuring using the following command:

```
./configure --help
```

4. Once `configure` is done, you can run `make` and `make install` to complete the installation.

    ```
    make -j 8 && make install
    ```

    The -j option specifies parallel jobs. Define this value based on your CPU cores, which can be utilized for the compilation job.

    Basically, `make` prepares builds all the libraries and binaries for PostgreSQL and `make install` copies all the necessary libraries and binaries to the installation location (could be default location or the location specified through the "--prefix" option).

5. Verify that all the binaries and libraries are installed and they are in the location that you have specified.

6. Once the installation is done, create a data directory where data can be stored. It is recommended to create a "postgres" OS user to own that data directory and Postgres Services.

    Each instance of PostgreSQL is referred to as a "cluster." It just means that an instance can have multiple databases. Please don't get confused with a cluster of multiple server nodes. Each data directory contains all data and configuration files of one instance. So, each instance can be referred to in two ways:

- Location of the data directory

- Port number

A single server can have many installations, and you can create multiple clusters using initdb.

Here are the commands that need to be executed to create a user, create a data directory, and initialize that data directory (assuming you have installed it in default locations):

```
adduser postgres
mkdir /usr/local/pgsql/data
chown postgres /usr/local/pgsql/data
su - postgres
/usr/local/pgsql/bin/initdb -D /usr/local/pgsql/data
```

Note "/usr/local/pgsql/data" is the data directory. initdb is the binary to initialize a new data directory.

In order to start the PostgreSQL, we should specify the associated data directory. Use the pg_ctl tool and specify the data directory to start the instance as follows:

```
/usr/local/pgsql/bin/pg_ctl -D /usr/local/pgsql/
data start
```

Details of basic requirements, installation procedure, postinstallation steps, and supported platforms are here: www.postgresql.org/docs/current/static/installation.html.

The complete build from source code and installation can be scripted as a simple shell script.

We are going to see a sample shell script that does source build and setup for you. This script file can be executed with three parameters to specify OS type, PostgreSQL version, and port number

For example, if we want to build PostgreSQL 11.4 on Linux and set up the instance on default port 5432, we use following command line:

```
sh <scriptfile> Linux 11.4 5432
```

Here is the content of the script file:

```
#!/bash/sh
export OS=$1
export VERSION=$2
export PORT=$3
export INSTALL_DIR=$HOME/pg_software

if [ ! -d "$INSTALL_DIR" ]
then
    echo "$INSTALL_DIR directory doesn't exist. Creating now"
    mkdir $INSTALL_DIR
    echo "$INSTALL_DIR directory created"
else
    echo "$INSTALL_DIR exists"
fi
```

```
cd $HOME/pg_software

## Downloading the source code as per OS

if [ "$1" == "Linux" ] || [ "$1" == "linux" ]; then
      echo "Downloading PostgreSQL $VERSION.."
   wget https://ftp.postgresql.org/pub/source/v$VERSION/
   postgresql-$VERSION.tar.bz2 >/dev/null
   if [ "$?" -gt "0" ]; then
      echo "Could not download the file, check if wget is
      installed or not"
      exit
    else
      echo "Downloaded PostgreSQL $VERSION..."
   fi
elif [ "$1" == "Mac" ] || [ "$1" == "mac" ]; then
      echo "Downloading PostgreSQL $VERSION.."
   curl -O https://ftp.postgresql.org/pub/source/v$VERSION/
   postgresql-$VERSION.tar.bz2 > $HOME/pg_software/
   comile_$VERSION.log 2>&1
   if [ "$?" -gt "0" ]; then
       echo "Could not download the file, check if curl is
       installed or not"
      exit
   else
      echo "Downloaded PostgreSQL $VERSION..."
   fi
else
      echo "currenly it works with linux and mac OSes"
   exit
fi
```

Compiling the source code

```
echo "wait ! let it compile..."
cd $INSTALL_DIR/
tar -xf postgresql-$VERSION.tar.bz2
cd postgresql-$VERSION
./configure --prefix=$HOME/pg_software/$VERSION && make world
-j 8 && make install-world > $HOME/compile.log
if [ "$?" -gt "0" ]; then
        echo "Could not compile the source, please look at
        compile.log for more information"
        exit
else
        echo "Ok, compiled it for you !!.."
fi
```

Setting up evn

```
echo "setting up env...it makes your life easy.. "

touch $HOME/pg_software/$VERSION/source_$VERSION.env
echo "export PATH=$HOME/pg_software/$VERSION/bin:$PATH" >>
$HOME/pg_software/$VERSION/source.env
echo "export PGPORT=5432" >> $HOME/pg_software/$VERSION/source.env
echo "export PGDATA=$HOME/pg_software/$VERSION/data" >> $HOME/
pg_software/$VERSION/source.env
echo "export PGDATABASE=postgres" >> $HOME/pg_
software/$VERSION/source.env
echo "export PGUSER=postgres" >> $HOME/pg_software/$VERSION/
source.env

echo "source $HOME/pg_software/$VERSION/source.env" >> $HOME/.
bash_profile
. $HOME/.bash_profile
```

```
echo "Ok, done with env setup.. now you can be lazy.. !"
## Create DATA directory

echo "Oh, it's data time.. creating data directory...!"

initdb -D $PGDATA -U postgres >/dev/null 2>&1

echo "Done buddy !! .. let me enable logging and allow
connections from other hosts....."
## Enable logging.. and allow other hosts.

echo "port=$PORT" >> $PGDATA/postgresql.conf
echo "logging_collector=on" >> $PGDATA/postgresql.conf
echo "listen_addresses='*'" >> $PGDATA/postgresql.conf

## Start database
echo "you are having coffee !!!.. Ok, np, let me start it for you..!"
pg_ctl -D $PGDATA start >/dev/null
sleep 5
echo "hmm.. seems it started.. but let me check once.."
## check DB is up

psql -p $PGPORT -U $PGUSER -d $PGDATABASE -c "select 1;" > /dev/null

if [ "$?" -gt "0" ]; then
      echo "Sorry !!, it's not started.. I'm not yet smart
      enough to fix.. :-(.. blame the author !!.."
else
      echo "hurray.. it works.. enjoy!"
fi
```

Binary Installation

This installation is nothing but downloading already compiled binaries
(from source installation) from different repositories maintained by
communities and PostgreSQL support vendors.

Binary installation expects the server to satisfy all the dependencies. However, most of the package managers are smart enough to detect the required dependencies and install them if required.

Some of the notable binary repositories are:

www.postgresql.org/ftp/binary/

https://yum.postgresql.org/

www.postgresql.org/download/linux/ubuntu/

RPM Installation

PostgreSQL maintains a repository where you can see all versions of PostgreSQL: https://yum.postgresql.org/rpmchart.php.

RHEL, CentOS, Oracle Enterprise Linux, and Scientific Linux are currently supported by the PostgreSQL yum repository. Only the current version of Fedora is supported due to a shorter support cycle, so Fedora is not recommended for any business critical server deployments.

You need to add and update the PostgreSQL repository maintained by the PostgreSQL Global Development Group (PGDG) to install a particular version of PostgreSQL RPMs. You can select a version of PostgreSQL and operating system at www.postgresql.org/download/linux/redhat/ to update your repository, as shown in the following screenshot.

To use the PostgreSQL Yum Repository, follow these steps:

1. Select version:

11	⇕

2. Select platform:

RedHat Enterprise, CentOS, Scientific or Oracle version 8	⇕

3. Select architecture:

x86_64	⇕

4. Install the repository RPM:

```
dnf install https://download.postgresql.org/pub/repos/yum/reporpms/EL-8-x86_64/pgdg-redhat-repo-latest.noarch.rpm
```

5. Install the client packages:

```
dnf install postgresql11
```

6. Optionally install the server packages:

```
dnf install postgresql11-server
```

Figure 1-1. *rpm installation*

Let us add and update the repository and install RPMs.

Note   PostgreSQL 11 and RHEL 8 are used to show demo.

---

1. To add and update the pgdg repository to get PostgreSQL 11, run the following command:

   ```
   dnf install https://download.postgresql.org/
   pub/repos/yum/reporpms/EL-8-x86_64/pgdg-
   redhat-repo-latest.noarch.rpm
   ```

2. To install only client packages:

   ```
   dnf install postgresql11
   ```

3. To install the server packages:

   ```
   dnf install postgresql11-server
   ```

4. To initialize the database and enable automatic start:

   ```
   /usr/pgsql-11/bin/postgresql-11-setup initdb
   systemctl enable postgresql-11
   systemctl start postgresql-11
   ```

5. To install language RPMs like Perl, Python, Tcl, etc., use the following command:

   ```
   dnf install postgresql11-plperl*
   dnf install postgresql11-plpython*
   dnf install postgresql11-pltcl*
   ```

6. Postinstallation

Automatic startup or auto-initialization of data directory is not enabled for Red Hat family distributions due to some policies. So, you need to perform the following steps manually to complete your database installation.

For RHEL / CentOS / SL / OL 6
```
service postgresql initdb
chkconfig postgresql on
```
For RHEL / CentOS / SL / OL 7, 8 Or Fedora 29 And Later Derived Distributions:
```
postgresql-setup initdb
systemctl enable postgresql.service
systemctl start postgresql.service
```

One-Click Installers for Linux, Windows, and Mac

The easiest way to install PostgreSQL is through installers. One-click installers provide a graphical wizard for installation. These installers have options to choose your installation and data directory locations, port, user, passwords, etc.

Download the installers from here (according to your OS): www.enterprisedb.com/downloads/postgres-postgresql-downloads.

Double-click the installer and follow the GUI wizard, where you can follow the simple steps to provide basic information of installation location, data directory, and port.

Plan for the Installation

We have discussed types of PostgreSQL installation and how to install it on different types of operating systems in the preceding section. However, how do you plan for the installation?

To plan for the installation, you need to analyze the answers to questions in the "Information Needed for Installation" section. So, note down:

Q1.   What is the operating system? What is the architecture of the OS (32/64 bit)?

If it is Linux:

You can go for any kind of installation that was discussed in the "Types of Installations" section. However, RPM installation is recommended because it is easy to update the repository and run a few commands to install and set up the database. For source and binary installations, you need to take care of dependencies manually, which will be a huge task if you have a server with minimal installation due to security reasons. For an installer installation you need a GUI, which will not be allowed in a few servers.

If it is Mac or Windows:

You can go for installer installation using a GUI. However, it is recommended to avoid installation on Mac in production environments.

Q2.   What are the machine specifications (CPU, RAM)?

Based on the amount of RAM on the server, you
can set the kernel level parameters before/after
installation. We will be covering more about what
parameters need to be changed and what are the
values in the "Tuning OS Parameters" section.

Q3.   What is the current size and expected growth of the
application?

Based on the current size and expected growth,
storage needs to be provisioned before you install
and set up the server. Once you get the filesystems
ready with the required storage, you can start with
the installation. It is difficult to increase the storage
without getting a down time of the database. So,
setting up storage at the time of installation will save
a lot of time in future.

Q4.   What filesystem is being used by the server?

PostgreSQL is best to work with the ext4 filesystem.
So, make sure you have the ext4 filesystem on the
server before installation. Sometimes, it will save a
lot of time in figuring out the performance issues
with the database.

Note   You need to benchmark the results and see which filesystem
is the best fit for your work loads.

Q5.   How many mount points?

It is recommended to create multiple mount points for PostgreSQL to avoid IO bottlenecks in future. We will discuss more about what can be distributed across mount points in the "General Recommendations for PostgreSQL Disk/Storage" section.

Q6.   Is public Internet accessible from the server?

If you have public Internet access on the server, your job will be easy. You can download source/binaries/rpms directly on the server and install them.

If you do not have public Internet access on the server, download source/binaries/rpms on a bastion/jump machine that has public access and copy it to a production server through a private network.

Once you have noted all the details, prepare documentation and follow the procedure to install the PostgreSQL.

General Recommendations for PostgreSQL Disk/Storage

Installation of PostgreSQL is a combined effort of database, system, and storage admins. Database administrators (DBAs) must work closely with the system and storage administrators. PostgreSQL relies heavily on the host OS for storage management. It does not have the ASM kind of features of Oracle for storage management.

Here are some recommendations to standardize and simplify PostgreSQL database installations.

Choose the Right Location and Ownership

Most people go for the default location to install the PostgreSQL binaries. However, you can install them in a specific location if you want, so that they will not be mixed with OS stuff. As discussed in the "Types of Installations" section, you can choose any custom location for installation. It is a good practice to have a base directory like "/opt/PostgreSQL" and differentiate versions using the first two digits in the version number, like "/opt/PostgreSQL/11/." It helps you to keep track of the binaries version during an upgrade the database in future.

It is recommended to have a separate OS user for PostgreSQL installation, "postgres", for example, and make it the owner of PostgreSQL installation.

One Cluster and Database per Server

In PostgreSQL, there are objects that are cluster specific and database specific. The following physical and logical objects are applicable at cluster wide within a PostgreSQL instance.

- Configuration files

- WAL (online and archived) files

- Tablespaces

- User accounts and roles

- Server log file

An older style of database object separation was through the use of multiple databases. An alternate and more manageable method to separate database objects within a single database server is through the use of schemas. However, too many schemas with a large number of tables may have an adverse effect on autovacuum.

To separate PostgreSQL clusters within a server, different data areas and IP port numbers need to be used. However, the virtualization capabilities of the OSes like Solaris's zones and FreeBSD jails or hypervisors like Xen and KVM make creation of multiple clusters within a single host unnecessary. The recommendation is to have only one PostgreSQL cluster per virtualized host.

FileSystem Layouts

We talked about mount points in the "Information Needed for Installation" section. PostgreSQL writes into multiple files, depending on the transaction that you execute. Following are the files that get updated:

- Data files
- WAL files
- Log files
- Temp files
- Tablespaces

To distribute the IO when updating these files, it is recommended to have these different kinds of files in different mount points. Let us look at how to do it.

Data Cluster Separation

While creating a data cluster, you can choose a mount point on which you want your data to reside. While initializing the cluster, use the -D option to mention data directory location or use the PGDATA variable to specify location. For example:

```
initdb -D /filesystem/for/data
```

WAL Files Separation

You can have a separate mount point for WAL files, as these are files will get updated on each transaction that modifies the database. There is no configuration parameter that does this separation directly. Every data cluster has a directory named "pg_xlog" (<= 9.6 version) or "pg_wal" (>=10 version). You can create a directory in the mount point that you want to assign for WAL files and create a symlink from pg_xlog or pg_wal directory to the new directory created.

Note   This change needs a restart of PostgreSQL. Once a symlink is created and PostgreSQL is restarted, you can see new WAL files generated in a new location. You can consider copying WALs from an old location to the new location before restarting PostgreSQL.

Log Files Separation

Log files are essential to start troubleshooting database issues. The amount of logging is based on the log settings in the configuration file. If you want to log everything for critical database systems, there can be huge log generation. So, separating log files into another mount point than data saves some IO pressure. You can do that using the "log_directory" parameter. This change just requires a reload of cluster. You can use the following steps:

```
postgres=# show log_directory ;
 log_directory
---------------
 log
(1 row)

postgres=# alter system set log_directory TO '/path/to/log/
filesystem';
```

```
ALTER SYSTEM
postgres=# select pg_reload_conf();
 pg_reload_conf
----------------
 t
(1 row)

postgres=# show log_directory ;
      log_directory
--------------------------
 /path/to/log/filesystem
(1 row)

postgres=#
```

Temp Files Separation

PostgreSQL uses temp files for the sorting operation in a query if allocated work memory is not sufficient. By default, it creates temp files in the "pgsql_tmp" directory under $PGDATA/base. However, you can create a tablespace and use it for temp file operations. You can use the following steps.

```
postgres=# show temp_tablespaces ;
 temp_tablespaces
-------------------

(1 row)

postgres=# create tablespace for_temp_files location '/tmp';
CREATE TABLESPACE
postgres=#
postgres=# alter system set temp_tablespaces to '/tmp';
ALTER SYSTEM
postgres=#
postgres=# select pg_reload_conf();
```

```
 pg_reload_conf
----------------
 t
(1 row)

postgres=# show temp_tablespaces ;
 temp_tablespaces
------------------
 "/tmp"
(1 row)

postgres=#
```

Tablespaces

Data directory is not the only location to store the postgres data; however, you can choose a different mount point to store the data. For that, you need to create a tablespace and assign it to the object that you want to move from the default data location to a new location. Or you can assign the tablespace to the user or database level so that all objects created by the user or all objects that are created inside the database will be stored under the mount point for which a tablespace is created. You can create a tablespace and assign objects using the following steps:

```
postgres=# create tablespace new_tblsc location '/Users/shbaji/
pg_software/newtblsc';
CREATE TABLESPACE
postgres=#
postgres=# alter table orders_1 set tablespace new_tblsc;
ALTER TABLE
postgres=#
postgres=# select relname, reltablespace from pg_class where
relname='orders_1';
```

```
relname | reltablespace
----------+---------------
 orders_1 |          33888
(1 row)

postgres=# select oid, spcname from pg_tablespace where
spcname='new_tblsc';
  oid  | spcname
-------+-----------
 33888 | new_tblsc
(1 row)

postgres=#
```

Tuning OS Parameters

Tuning of OS parameters is divided as:

- Before installation

- After installation

Before Installation

The first thing you need to look for before you start installing PostgreSQL is shared memory parameters. As PostgreSQL uses shared memory, you may need to alter kernel parameters like SHMMAX, SHMMIN, SHMALL, etc. For new versions from PostgreSQL 9.3, you may not need to do it, as it uses POSIX memory allocation.

If you don't change, PostgreSQL installation can exhaust resource limits quickly.

You can change parameters according to your PostgreSQL parameter settings. PostgreSQL shared memory usage is as follows:

Name	Description	Values Needed to Run One PostgreSQL Instance
SHMMAX	Maximum size of shared memory segment (bytes)	At least 1kB, but the default is usually much higher
SHMMIN	Minimum size of shared memory segment (bytes)	1
SHMALL	Total amount of shared memory available (bytes or pages)	Same as SHMMAX if bytes, or ceil (SHMMAX/PAGE_SIZE) if pages, plus room for other applications
SHMSEG	Maximum number of shared memory segments per process	Only one segment is needed, but the default is much higher.
SHMMNI	Maximum number of shared memory segments system-wide	Like SHMSEG plus room for other applications
SEMMNI	Maximum number of semaphore identifiers (i.e., sets)	At least ceil((max_connections + autovacuum_max_workers + max_wal_senders + max_worker_processes + 5) / 16) plus room for other applications
SEMMNS	Maximum number of semaphores system-wide	Ceil((max_connections + autovacuum_max_workers + max_wal_senders + max_worker_processes + 5) / 16) * 17 plus room for other applications
SEMMSL	Maximum number of semaphores per set	At least 17
SEMMAP	Number of entries in semaphore map	See text
SEMVMX	Maximum value of semaphore	At least 1000 (The default is often 32767; do not change unless necessary.)

According to usage of PostgreSQL as shown in the preceding table, you can change the kernel parameters using the following table (it is applicable <= PostgreSQL 9.2):

Usage	Approximate shared memory bytes required (as of 8.3)
Connections	(1800 + 270 * max_locks_per_transaction) * max_connections
Autovacuum workers	(1800 + 270 * max_locks_per_transaction) * autovacuum_max_workers
Prepared transactions	(770 + 270 * max_locks_per_transaction) * max_prepared_transactions
Shared disk buffers	(block_size + 208) * shared_buffers
WAL buffers	(wal_block_size + 8) * wal_buffers
Fixed space requirements	770 kB

If you are changing these parameters, keep in mind that you will have to reload the settings using "sysctl -p." You can even change these in runtime.

After Installation

Here are the parameters that you can tune in a server where PostgreSQL is running.

- overcommit_memory

- overcommit_ratio

- vm.dirty_ratio

- vm.dirty_background_ratio

- THP (Transparent Huge Pages)

- HP (Huge Pages)

Before you set any of these parameters, you should understand exactly what these parameters are and what benefit would you get from setting them. As it comes more under "configuration," we will cover these parameters in Chapter 2.

Troubleshooting Installation Issues

Here are a few things you should note for installations, as they help in troubleshooting:

- In source installation, most of the issues come while building. Most common issues are missing libraries like readline or zlib. You can manually install those libraries and try recompiling.

- Configure creates a compilation log where you can see issues related to missing libraries and tools.

- In RPM installation, you have to update the repository first and then try installation; otherwise you may not be able to find the version you are trying to install.

- In a GUI installer-based installation, log files will be created under a /tmp location. These are bitrock installers, so, you can see log files with bitrock_xx.log, for example.

Summary

In this chapter, we talked about types of PostgreSQL installation procedures and how to work with them. We also covered what information you would need from the customer to plan for the installation, and some general recommendations you should follow to set up a best environment. We also covered, pre/post installation steps and some troubleshooting procedures. In the next chapter, we talk about configuring the postgres, as default settings come with wide compatibility. We will cover what areas can be set to improve PostgreSQL performance.

CHAPTER 2

Configure Your Database for Better Performance

In the last chapter, we talked about information that needed to be gathered for PostgreSQL installation, and planning installation based on that information. Also, we covered types of PostgreSQL installations, pre/post-installation tuning, troubleshooting procedures, and some general recommendations to consider during installation to avoid performance issues in future. In this chapter, we will cover some initial postinstallation steps for beginners, all important configuration files and their uses and their default settings, recommendations to tune configuration files, and OS parameters tuning for performance improvement.

Initial Steps After Installation

Let us start with some initial steps right after the installation. These steps are differentiated between PostgreSQL developers and administrators.

© Baji Shaik 2020

B. Shaik, *PostgreSQL Configuration*, https://doi.org/10.1007/978-1-4842-5663-3_2

For PostgreSQL Developers

Once PostgreSQL is installed by admins, developers need a client tool to connect PostgreSQL and do their development work. The most popular client tool for PostgreSQL is pgAdmin. This tool is from the PostgreSQL community. You can download this tool from `http://pgadmin.org`.

Note   There are many client tools that you can use for PostgreSQL. All available tools are in PostgreSQL Clients (`https://wiki.postgresql.org/wiki/PostgreSQL_Clients`).

After you download and install pgAdmin, the window looks like Figure 2-1.

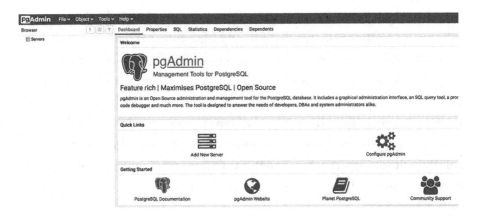

Figure 2-1. *pgAdmin home*

Now you need to add your database to connect. If you right-click the servers, you can see the Create Server option, as shown in Figure 2-2.

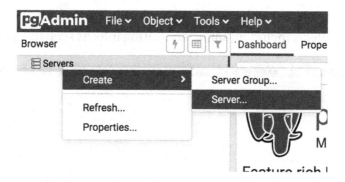

Figure 2-2. *Create server*

Enter a name for the server that you want to add, and database details and credentials as per installation and setup provided by the admin in the connection section, as seen in Figure 2-3.

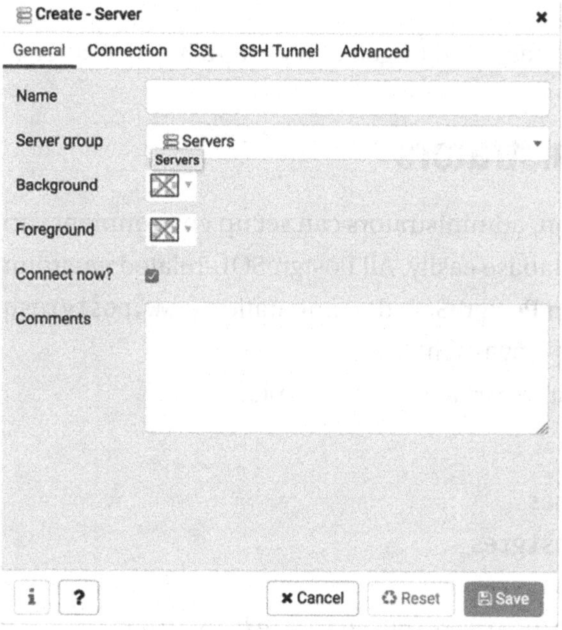

Figure 2-3. *Provide database details*

After you connect with your database details, you can see the databases/objects including some monitoring info, as seen in Figure 2-4.

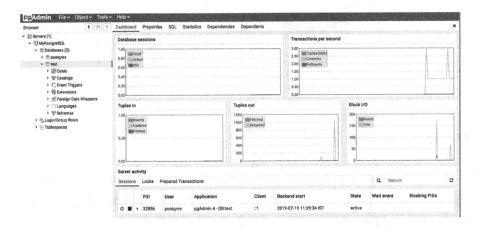

Figure 2-4. *Database status*

That is a bit basic and targeted to PostgreSQL beginners.

For Administrators

After installation, administrators can set up environment variables to connect the database easily. All PostgreSQL-related environment variables are described in PostgreSQL documentation (`www.postgresql.org/ docs/11/libpq-envars.html`).

Here are some variables, for example:

```
PGPORT=5432
PGUSER=postgres
PGPASSWORD=postgres
PGDATABASE=postgres
PGDATA=/Users/username/pg_software/9.6.9/data
```

You can export these into your bash_profile, including PostgreSQL binary location. Administrators use psql client to connect the database. Psql client can read a file named ".psqlrc" automatically. So, admins can set up some monitoring queries in this file to see the information as soon as they connect. This file should be placed in the PostgreSQL user's home directory. Here is a sample output you see if you set up the ".psqlrc" file.

```
$ cat .psqlrc
\set QUIET ON

\set PROMPT1 '%[%033[1;32;40m%]%M:%>; %n@%/%[%033[0m%]% # '
\set PAGER OFF
\set HISTSIZE 2000
\set ECHO_HIDDEN ON
\set COMP_KEYWORD_CASE upper

\timing
\encoding unicode

\pset null 'NULL'
\pset border 2

\set QUIET OFF

\echo '\nCurrent Host Server Date Time : '`date` '\n'

\echo 'Administrative queries:\n'
\echo '\t\t\t:settings\t-- Server Settings'
\echo '\t\t\t:conninfo\t-- Server connections'
\echo '\t\t\t:activity\t-- Server activity'
\echo '\t\t\t:locks\t\t-- Lock info'
\echo '\t\t\t:waits\t\t-- Waiting queires'
\echo '\t\t\t:uptime\t\t-- Server uptime'
\echo '\t\t\t:menu\t\t-- Help Menu'
\echo '\t\t\t\\h\t\t-- Help with SQL commands'
\echo '\t\t\t\\?\t\t-- Help with psql commands\n'
```

```
\echo 'Development queries:\n'
\echo '\t\t\t:sp\t\t-- Current Search Path'
\echo '\t\t\t:clear\t\t-- Clear screen'
\echo '\t\t\t:ll\t\t-- List\n'
```

-- Administration queries

```
\set menu '\\i ~/.psqlrc'
```

```
\set settings 'select name, setting,unit,context from pg_settings;'
```

```
\set locks  'SELECT bl.pid AS blocked_pid, a.usename AS
blocked_user, kl.pid AS blocking_pid, ka.usename AS blocking_
user, a.query AS blocked_statement FROM pg_catalog.pg_locks
bl JOIN pg_catalog.pg_stat_activity a ON bl.pid = a.pid JOIN
pg_catalog.pg_locks kl JOIN pg_catalog.pg_stat_activity ka
ON kl.pid = ka.pid ON bl.transactionid = kl.transactionid AND
bl.pid != kl.pid WHERE NOT bl.granted;'
```

```
\set conninfo 'select usename, count(*) from pg_stat_activity
group by usename;'
```

```
\set activity 'select datname, pid, usename, application_
name,client_addr, client_hostname, client_port, query, state
from pg_stat_activity;'
```

```
\set waits 'SELECT datname, usename, wait_event_type, wait_
event, pg_blocking_pids(pid) AS blocked_by, query FROM pg_stat_
activity WHERE wait_event IS NOT NULL;'
```

```
\set uptime 'select now() - pg_postmaster_start_time() AS uptime;'
```

-- Development queries:

```
\set sp 'SHOW search_path;'
\set clear '\\! clear;'
\set ll '\\! ls -lrt;'
```

You can see the information as shown in Figure 2-5 when you connect to psql with the preceding ".psqlrc" file.

```
8c85902e3a2c:~ shbaji$ psql

Current Host Server Date Time : Fri Jul 19 12:19:56 IST 2019

Administrative queries:

                        :settings        -- Server Settings
                        :conninfo        -- Server connections
                        :activity        -- Server activity
                        :locks           -- Lock info
                        :waits           -- Waiting queires
                        :uptime          -- Server uptime
                        :menu            -- Help Menu
                        \h               -- Help with SQL commands
                        \?               -- Help with psql commands

Development queries:

                        :sp              -- Current Search Path
                        :clear           -- Clear screen
                        :ll              -- List

psql (10.2)
Type "help" for help.

[local]:5411; postgres@postgres #
```

Figure 2-5. *psqlrc info*

Configuration Files and Recommendations

Let us briefly talk about PostgreSQL configuration files. There are three cluster configuration files that we should know about while working with PostgreSQL. Those are the postgresql.conf, pg_hba.conf, and pg_ident. conf files.

postgresql.conf

This is the main configuration file of PostgreSQL. All settings related to PostgreSQL behavior with regard to auditing, authentication, logging, performance, etc. are configured through this configuration file. The default location of this file is under the $PGDATA (data directory) location; however, it can be customized through the "config_file" parameter. To know the location of your configuration file, just type "show config_file;" in the psql terminal.

```
[local]:5411; postgres@postgres # show config_file;
+------------------------------------------------------------------+
|                           config_file                            |
+------------------------------------------------------------------+
| /Users/shbaji/pg_software/10.2/bin/../data/postgresql.conf |
+------------------------------------------------------------------+
(1 row)

Time: 1.721 ms
```

Note   A parameter setting in postgres.conf can be overridden by the next setting. So, if you have a duplicate setting of a parameter in the file, the bottom one always will be in effect.

Depending on the parameter, you would need to reload or restart the database accordingly. You will find which parameter needs reload and which needs restart using the following query:

```
SELECT name, context FROM pg_settings WHERE name = '<parameter_
value>';
```

If the value of context is "postmaster" it needs a restart of the database. For all other values, it is just a reload.

pg_hba.conf

Client authentication will be controlled by this file. You can control from which server you want connections to the database and in which way. The default location of this file is the $PGDATA directory; however, this can be changed using the "hba_file" parameter in the postgresql.conf file.

```
[local]:5411; postgres@postgres # show hba_file ;
+-------------------------------------------------------+
|                       hba_file                        |
+-------------------------------------------------------+
| /Users/shbaji/pg_software/10.2/bin/../data/pg_hba.conf |
+-------------------------------------------------------+
(1 row)

Time: 3.434 ms
```

Note   This file is read from top to bottom for the first match of the rule. If you have similar lines with different authentication methods or different IP ranges, the top one will be picked up.

Changing this file needs a reload of the database.

Records in this file can have one of these seven formats:

```
local     database   user auth-method  [auth-options]
host      database   user address auth-method  [auth-options]
hostssl   database   user address auth-method  [auth-options]
hostnossl database   user address auth-method  [auth-options]
host      database   user IP-address IP-mask   auth-method
                                                [auth-options]
hostssl   database   user IP-address  IP-mask  auth-method
                                                [auth-options]
hostnossl database   user IP-address  IP-mask  auth-method
                                                [auth-options]
```

Detailed information on this file is available in PostgreSQL documentation: www.postgresql.org/docs/current/auth-pg-hba-conf.html.

pg_ident.conf

PostgreSQL provides ident-based authentication. It works by obtaining the client's operating system username and using it as the allowed database username with an optional username mapping. When we use an external authentication system, the system username might not be the same as database username. To allow external authentication, we should map the system username with the database username, and we can also set a map name to hide the system username and database username-related details. The default location of this file in under the $PGDATA directory and can be changed using the "ident_file" parameter in the postgresql.conf file.

If you open your pg_ident.conf file, you will find the following line at the bottom of the file:

```
# MAPNAME        SYSTEM-USERNAME        PG-USERNAME
```

You can add value to map system username and database username:

```
# MAPNAME        SYSTEM-USERNAME        PG-USERNAME
User123          LinuxUser              PGUser
```

Once you map your system user and database user in the pg_ident. conf file, you can use the map name in the pg_hba.conf file to allow external authentication.

Go to your PostgreSQL data directory and open a pg_hba.conf file. You can add the map name of the system user and database user in the METHOD column. For example:

```
# TYPE  DATABASE     USER     ADDRESS          METHOD
host    all          all      127.0.0.0/16     ident map=User123
```

Parameter Recommendations

PostgreSQL ships with a basic configuration tuned for wide compatibility rather than performance. Although the default settings of PostgreSQL that come with the installation are viable, it is always recommended to tune some basic parameters according to your environment and application behavior.

Before you change any setting in the postgresql.conf file, you should know the types of settings and when they take effect.

The Types of Settings

There are several different types of configuration settings, divided up based on the possible inputs they can take:

- *Boolean*: true, false, on, off

- *Integer*: Whole numbers (2112)

- *Float*: Decimal values (21.12)

- *Memory / Disk*: Integers (2112) or "computer units" (512MB, 2112GB). Avoid integers—you need to know the underlying unit to figure out what they mean.

- *Time*: Time units, aka d, m, s (e.g., 30 s). Sometimes the unit is left out; don't do that.

- *Strings*: Single-quoted text ('pg_log')

- *ENUMs*: Strings, but from a specific list ('WARNING', 'ERROR')

- *Lists*: A comma-separated list of strings ("$user",public,tsearch2)

When They Take Effect

PostgreSQL settings have different levels of flexibility for when they can be changed, usually related to internal code restrictions. The complete list of levels is:

- *Postmaster*: Requires restart of server

- *SIGHUP*: Requires an HUP of the server, either by kill -HUP (usually -1), pg_ctl reload, or SELECT pg_reload_conf();

- *User*: Can be set within individual sessions; takes effect only within that session

- *Internal*: Set at compile time and can't be changed; mainly for reference

- *Backend*: Settings that must be set before session start

- *Superuser*: Can be set at runtime for the server by superusers

Tuning Tools

Instead of you analyzing your database manually, there are some tools available on the market that do it for you:

- postgresqltuner (`https://github.com/jfcoz/postgresqltuner`)

- pgBadger (`https://github.com/darold/pgbadger`)

  PGTune (`https://pgtune.leopard.in.ua/#/`)

- PostgreSQL Configuration Tool (`www.pgconfig.org/#/tuning`)

You can analyze your database using the tools listed, and they can come up with some tuning advice.

Review Parameters

We are not going to cover all the parameters here; however, there are a few parameters you must consider when you are setting up an environment for the first time. Let us divide the parameters into sections like:

- Connections related

- Memory related

- Planner/Cost related

- WAL related

- Autovacuum related

- Logging related

- Replication related

Let us look at each section and see what parameters can be changed.

Connections Related

All the documentation for connection or authentication-related parameters is here: www.postgresql.org/docs/current/runtime-config-connection.html.

listen_addresses

By default, PostgreSQL listens only on the loopback interface so that it responds to connections from the local host. If you want your server to be accessible from other systems via standard TCP/IP networking, you need to change listen_addresses from its default. The usual approach is to set it to listen on all network interfaces on the server by a setting like this:

```
listen_addresses = '*'
```

And then control who can and cannot connect via the pg_hba.conf file.

max_connections

The max_connections setting refers to the maximum number of client connections allowed. Before setting this parameter, you should ask your customer how many concurrent connections their application requests at peak point.

If the system being reviewed uses a connection pooler, there will likely be a predefined limit to the number of connections needed to the database. So, max_connections should not be much higher than this limit, but you will still need to take into account any superuser connections (defined by superuser_reserved_connections) and any nonpooled connections (such as those coming from reporting systems or scheduled tasks).

You should be careful before increasing this parameter, as increasing needs some memory setting as well, and it is explained in the "Before Installation" section of Chapter 1. Generally, PostgreSQL on good hardware can support a few hundred connections. If you want to have thousands instead, you should consider using connection pooling software to reduce the connection overhead, which we will discuss in the "Implementing Pooler" section of Chapter 7.

Memory Related

You can see all memory-related parameters at: `www.postgresql.org/docs/current/runtime-config-resource.html`.

We will discuss a few parameters for recommendations here.

shared_buffers

On Linux, there is a general rule of thumb that is used to determine a decent value for shared_buffers. It's recommended that it be set to a size 15% to 25% of total RAM. However, there is a point where the amount of shared memory used for buffering pages stops yielding noticeable benefits.

On versions of PostgreSQL prior to 8.4, the maximum value should be 2.5GB, otherwise the maximum should be dependent and should be decided after benchmark. Note that when using PostgreSQL 9.2 or earlier, kernel parameters may require adjustment to accommodate any changes in this parameter on later versions.

On Windows, the general advice is to cap shared_buffers at 512MB. This is based on benchmarks the PostgreSQL community has performed on it in the past. Increasing it beyond this size has not been confirmed as useful.

effective_cache_size

The effective_cache_size parameter should be set to an estimate of how much memory is available for disk caching by the operating system (page cache) and within the database itself, after considering what's used by the OS itself and other applications. This is a guideline for the SQL planner saying how much memory it should expect to be available in the OS and PostgreSQL buffer caches, but not an allocation. This value is used only by the PostgreSQL query planner to figure out whether plans it's considering would be expected to fit in RAM or not. If it's set too low, indexes may not be used for executing queries the expected way. The setting for shared_buffers is not considered here—only the effective_cache_size value is, so it should include memory dedicated to the database too.

This parameter can safely be set to a large value without any risk of running out of memory, as it's only used for query planning. In most cases this should be 75% of RAM.

work_mem

This parameter is useful when SQL statements use a lot of complex sorts. This allows PostgreSQL to do operations in in-memory, due to which execution time will be reduced.

Increasing work_mem can lead to far less disk swapping, and therefore far quicker queries. However, it can cause problems if set too high, and should be constrained taking into account max_connections. The following calculation is what is typically recommended to determine a decent work_mem value:

```
Total RAM * 0.25 / max_connections
```

If there are large reporting queries that run on the database that require more work memory than a typical connection, work_mem can be set for those particular queries. If, for example, there is a reporting user that only runs infrequent but large reports, a specific work_mem setting can be applied to that particular user/role.

For example:

```
ALTER ROLE reporting SET work_mem = '64MB';
```

maintenance_work_mem

This specifies the maximum amount of memory to be used by maintenance operations, such as VACUUM, CREATE INDEX, and ALTER TABLE ADD FOREIGN KEY. It's important that maintenance_work_mem be given enough memory so that VACUUM processes can complete their work more quickly by working in larger batches. We typically recommend 1/20th of RAM (or Total RAM * 0.05). Note that this has to be balanced against the number of autovacuum_max_workers, as each autovacuum worker allocates maintenance_work_mem size of memory. Otherwise, if on a 64GB system you had:

```
maintenance_work_mem = 3GB
autovacuum_max_workers = 20
```

This would likely exhaust available memory (3GB * 20 = 60GB), assuming the database cluster was large enough for autovacuum processes to make use of all the memory. So this should then be balanced out:

```
maintenance_work_mem = 400MB
autovacuum_max_workers = 20
```

Resulting in 8GB (400MB * 20) being used, which would be much more reasonable on a 64GB system. To factor this into your calculation, you may wish to use something like the following:

Total RAM * 0.15 / autovacuum_max_workers

It's worth noting that other processes can still request maintenance_work_mem to build indexes and in setting up foreign keys, so there needs to be some additional headroom.

Planner/Cost Related

All query planner-related parameters are here: www.postgresql.org/docs/current/runtime-config-query.html.

You can set few parameters as hints to the query planner so that it changes plan accordingly. So, all parameters starting with "enable_" refer to hints.

```
[local]:5411; postgres@postgres # select name, setting from
pg_settings where name like 'enable_%';
```

name	setting
enable_bitmapscan	on
enable_gathermerge	on
enable_hashagg	on
enable_hashjoin	on
enable_indexonlyscan	on
enable_indexscan	on
enable_material	on
enable_mergejoin	on
enable_nestloop	on

```
| enable_seqscan         | on        |
| enable_sort            | on        |
| enable_tidscan         | on        |
+-----------------------+---------+
(12 rows)
```

seq_page_cost

This represents the estimated cost of a disk fetch as part of sequential scan. The optimizer picks a plan depending on cost-related parameters. So, this is one of the parameters you should consider for tuning. You should be careful while modifying the value of this parameter, as the planner picks different plans sometimes depending on the value.

It's recommended to tune this parameter if you are using SSD for storage.

random_page_cost

This setting suggests to the optimizer how long it will take your disks to seek a random disk page, as a multiple of how long a sequential read (with a cost of 1.0) takes. If you have particularly fast disks, as commonly found with RAID arrays of SCSI disks, it may be appropriate to lower random_page_cost, which will encourage the query optimizer to use random access index scans. Some feel that 4.0 is always too large on current hardware; it's not unusual for administrators to standardize on always setting this between 2.0 and 3.0 instead. In some cases that behavior is a holdover from earlier PostgreSQL versions, where having random_page_cost too high was more likely to screw up plan optimization than it is now (and setting at or below 2.0 was regularly necessary). Since these cost estimates are just that—estimates—it shouldn't hurt to try lower values.

But this is not where you should start to search for plan problems. Note that random_page_cost is pretty far down this list (at the end in fact). If you are getting bad plans, this shouldn't be the first thing you look at, even though lowering this value may be effective. Instead, you should start by making sure autovacuum is working properly, that you are collecting enough statistics, and that you have correctly sized the memory parameters for your server—all the things just gone over. After you've done all those much more important things, if you're still getting bad plans, then you should see if lowering random_page_cost is still useful.

cpu_tuple_cost

This is the cost of processing each row. The default is 0.01, but previous performance benefits have been seen setting this to 0.03, which can result in better query plans. This is particularly relevant to systems where the database(s) fit in memory and CPU utilization is high

WAL Related

Documentation for all WAL-related parameters is available here: www.postgresql.org/docs/current/runtime-config-wal.html.

wal_buffers

From PostgreSQL version 9.1 onward, the default for this is set to -1, which automatically sets it to 1/32nd of shared_buffers capped at 16MB. This is probably fine, but there have been performance benefits observed by setting this to 32MB, although no higher. It's recommended that this be no lower than 16MB, as it's a trivial amount of shared memory to reserve relative to shared_buffers.

wal_level

As we will always recommend that the customer uses point-in-time recovery, we suggest that wal_level be set to at least "archive." This will need to be set to "hot_standby" or "replica" for using streaming replication.

bgwriter_delay

The default for this setting is 200ms. This should be set to no lower than 10 ms, but on systems with a high volume of writes, it's a good idea to lower this from its default value to at least 100 ms.

bgwriter_lru_maxpages

This setting is set to a very conservative value of 100 by default, which means only 100 buffers are written in every round. This tends to get set to 1000 to ensure the background writer process can write a sizable amount of buffers in each round.

bgwriter_lru_multiplier

This is set to a default of 2, but on systems with a heavy write load, it may be beneficial to increase this to 3 or 4.

synchronous_commit

This is enabled by default, but if a customer is willing to risk the most recent changes to improve write throughput, this can be disabled. This is a safer alternative to disabling fsync. This can actually be set at the database level, so it can be disabled on databases where the risk of losing some data in a crash isn't a big deal but performance is. It can also be disabled for specific roles (such as those that perform bulk loading activities), or in individual sessions if such a dedicated role doesn't exist.

fsync

This should almost always be enabled, because if the system crashes without fsyncs occurring, the cluster will likely be corrupted. Some customers will claim that their storage system's battery-backed cache will solve any problems flushing changes to disk. While a lot of storage devices claim this, it cannot be the whole truth. If the customer is determined to keep this setting off, it may be worth suggesting they instead set synchronous_commit to "off," as this will yield a performance benefit without the risk of corruption, but will come with the risk of losing some of the most recent data.

effective_io_concurrency

If the database cluster's main storage system has multiple spindles, set effective_io_concurrency to match the number of spindles but don't include any parity drives. This can improve bitmap index scans by reading ahead when multiple indexes are used.

For example, if they are using four disks in RAID 10 (striped and mirrored), effective_io_concurrency should be 4. For SSDs and memory-backed storages, this value can be in hundreds.

checkpoint_segments

This parameter exists in < PostgreSQL 9.5 version. The default of 3 is always too low. Typically this should be set between 16 and 64 or 256; the busier the writes on the system are, the higher this number should be. If set too high, it can affect the impact of checkpoints and increase recovery times by an excessive amount.

checkpoint_timeout

The more checkpoint_segments there are, the more time will be needed to complete a checkpoint, so this should be somewhere in the 5 min to 15 min range. Note that increasing this timeout would increase recovery time.

checkpoint_completion_target

This default of 0.5 means that checkpoints will aim to complete in half the time defined by checkpoint_timeout. To reduce the IO impact of checkpoints, this should spread the checkpoint out to nearer to the timeout, so a value of 0.8 or 0.9 is typically recommended.

checkpoint_warning

This needs to be changed to consider the expected amount of time for a checkpoint to complete.

Autovacuum Related

All autovacuum-related parameters are here: www.postgresql.org/docs/current/runtime-config-autovacuum.html.

autovacuum

This should nearly always be set to "on," otherwise no autovacuuming will occur in the database and there will certainly need to be routine manual vacuums applied.

autovacuum_max_workers

The default of 3 tends to be too low for anything except small database systems. This should probably be set to something within the 6 to 12 range, leaning more toward the latter if there are a lot of tables with frequent updates or deletes.

autovacuum_naptime

The default of 1 min may be sufficient for some systems, but on busier ones with many writes it may be beneficial to increase this to stop autovacuum waking up too often.

Also, on systems with many databases, this should be increased because this setting determines the wake up time per database. An autovacuum worker process will begin as frequently as autovacuum_naptime / number of databases.

For example, if autovacuum_naptime = 1 min (60 seconds), and there were 60 databases, an autovacuum worker process would be started every second (60 seconds / 60 databases = 1 second).

However, tuning this setting too high can result in more work needed to be done in each vacuuming round.

autovacuum_vacuum_threshold / autovacuum_analyze_threshold

These both determine the minimum number of rows in a table that need to have changed in order for the table to be scheduled for an autovacuum and an autoanalyze, respectively. The default for both is 50, which is very low for most tables.

autovacuum_vacuum_scale_factor / autovacuum_analyze_scale_factor

These both determine the percentage of a table that needs to have changes in order for the table to be scheduled for an autovacuum and an autoanalyze, respectively. The default for the autovacuum_vacuum_scale_factor is 0.2 (meaning 20%), and autovacuum_analyze_scale_factor is 0.1 (meaning 10%). Both of these figures are fine for tables of a modest size (up to around 500MB), but for larger tables they are too high. If, for example, there was a table that was 120GB in size, 24GB (20% of 120GB) worth of dead tuples would have to exist before they can start being cleaned up, which would be a lot of vacuuming work once it kicks in. However, if large tables are in the minority on the database, it's better to set these parameters on the table level rather than in the config file.

autovacuum_vacuum_cost_delay

This defaults to 20 ms, which is very conservative and can prevent VACUUM from keeping up with changes. This should nearly always be decreased, and in many cases to as low as 2ms. It may need to be tested with various settings to see what's needed to keep up.

Logging Related

All logging-related parameters are here: www.postgresql.org/docs/ current/runtime-config-logging.html.

We will be covering a lot about logging in Chapter 5.

Replication Related

All replication-related parameters are here: www.postgresql.org/docs/ current/runtime-config-replication.html.

max_wal_senders

This must always be greater than the number of replicas. If the data is replicated to multiple sites, then multiple max_wal_senders come into play. So, it is important to ensure this parameter is set to an optimal number.

max_replication_slots

In general, all the data changes occurring on the tables are written to WAL files in pg_xlog / pg_wal, which are known as WAL records. The wal sender process would pick up those WAL records (belonging to the tables being replicated) and send across to the replicas, and the wal_receiver process on the replica site would apply those changes at the subscriber node.

The WAL files are removed from the pg_xlog/pg_wal location whenever a checkpoint occurs. If the WAL files are removed even before the changes are applied to the subscriber node, replication would break and lag behind. In case the subscriber node lags behind, a replication slot would ensure all the WAL files needed for the subscriber to get in sync with the provider are retained. It is recommended to configure one replication slot to each subscriber node.

max_worker_processes

It is important to have an optimal number of worker processors configured. This depends on the max number of processes a server can have. This is possible only in multi-CPU environments. Max_worker_processes will ensure multiple processes are spawned to get the job done in a faster way by utilizing multiple CPU cores. When replicating data using logical replication, this parameter can help generate multiple worker processes to replicate the data faster. There is a specific parameter called max_logical_worker_ processes that will ensure multiple processes are used to copy the data.

max_logical_worker_processes

This parameter specifies the maximum number of logical worker processes required to perform table data replication and synchronization. This value is taken from max_worker_processes, which should be higher than this parameter value. This parameter is very beneficial when replicating data to multiple sites in multi-CPU environments. The default is 4. The max value depends on how many worker processes the system supports.

max_sync_workers_per_subscription

This parameter specifies the maximum number of synchronization processes required per subscription. The synchronization process takes place during initial data sync and this parameter can be used to ensure that happens faster. Currently, only one synchronization process can be configured per table, which means multiple tables can be synced initially in parallel. The default value is 2. This value is picked from the max_ logical_worker_processes value.

OS Recommendations

As mentioned in the "After Installation" section in Chapter 1, here are the parameters that you can tune at Linux OS where PostgreSQL is running:

- overcommit_memory

- overcommit_ratio

- vm.dirty_ratio

- vm.dirty_background_ratio

- THP (Transparent Huge Pages)

- HP (Huge Pages)

Before we go for tuning, let us look at some definitions:

- *Virtual Memory*: The sum of all the RAM and SWAP in a given system. When speaking about memory in the context of this section, we are referring to virtual memory.

- *Overcommit*: Allocating more memory than available Virtual Memory

- *Allocate*: In the context of memory management, an allocation of memory can be considered a "promise" that the memory is available. The actually physical memory is not assigned until it is actually needed. This assignment is done at a page level. When a new page (normally 8KB) is needed, the system triggers a page fault.

Why Allow Overcommits?

The Linux virtual memory implementation uses several tactics to optimize the amount of memory used (one such strategy is called "Copy on Write" and is used when forking child processes). The result of this is that often less memory is actually used than is reported via the /proc filesystem (and by extension ps).

In this case, minor overcommits are acceptable, as normally sufficient memory is available to service this. However, this approach can result in memory being allocated when in truth not enough is free.

To handle this case, Linux supports several different overcommit strategies specified by an integer value for the vm.overcommit setting.

Overcommit Strategy 0

This is the default strategy that Linux uses. In this case, all of the virtual memory is available to the system for allocations and all allocations are granted unless they appear to require a significant overcommit.

If, when a page fault occurs, there is not enough memory available (i.e., we have an overcommit), the system will trigger an "Out of Memory Killer" (OOM Killer). The OOM Killer will select a process currently running on the system and terminate that process. It uses a set of heuristics to select the process to terminate. Note that it is usually not possible to predict when this process will be required, nor which processes will be selected for termination.

Overcommit Strategy 1

This strategy is normally reserved for systems running processes that will be allocating very large arrays that are sparsely populated. In this mode, any allocation will be successful. In the event that an overcommit is detected, the process that detects the overcommit will generate a memory error and fail catastrophically (no cleanup; process simply stops).

Please note that as memory is not assigned until needed, a process that fails is not necessarily the one that has allocated the most memory. Due to the nature of memory usage predicting which process will fail due to memory overcommits is not possible.

Overcommit Strategy 2

With this mode Linux performs strict memory accounting and will only grant an allocation if required memory is actually available. As this check is done at the time of allocation, the programme requesting the memory can deal with the failure gracefully (in the case of GPDB generating an "Out of Memory" error) and cleaning up the session that's encountered the error.

This strategy will also allocate a portion of the physical RAM strictly for kernel use. The amount restricted is configured by the setting vm.overcommit_ratio. This means the amount of virtual memory (over committable memory) available for programs is actually:

SWAP + (RAM ∗ (overcommit_ratio/100))

The reserved memory is used for things such as IO buffers and system calls.

Let's look at some numbers:

Scenario 1:

4 GB RAM, 4 GB Swap, overcommit_memory = 2, overcommit_ratio = 50

Memory Allocation Limit = 4 GB Swap Space + 4 GB RAM ∗ (50% Overcommit Ratio / 100)

Memory Allocation Limit = 6 GB

Scenario 2:

4 GB RAM, 8 GB Swap, overcommit_memory = 2, overcommit_ratio = 50

Memory Allocation Limit = 8 GB Swap Space + 4 GB RAM * (50% Overcommit Ratio / 100)

Memory Allocation Limit = 10 GB

Scenario 3:

4 GB RAM, 2 GB Swap, overcommit_memory = 2, overcommit_ratio = 50

Memory Allocation Limit = 2 GB Swap Space + 4 GB RAM * (50% Overcommit Ratio / 100)

Memory Allocation Limit = 4 GB

Note that this is the total amount of memory that Linux will allocate. This includes all running daemons and other applications. Don't assume that your application will be able to allocate the total limit. Linux will also provide the memory allocation limit in the field CommitLimit in /proc/meminfo.

vm.dirty_ratio

This determines the number of pages, as a percentage of total system memory, after which the pdflush background writeback daemon will start writing out dirty data. Default is 20. It's recommended that this be decreased to 2 to make flushes more frequent but result in fewer IO spikes.

vm.dirty_background_ratio

This determines the number of pages, as a percentage of available memory (including cache), that the pdflush background writeback daemon will start writing out dirty data. Default is 10. It's recommended this be decreased to 1 to make flushes more frequent but result in less IO.

THP

It is always recommended to disable THP on a Linux system for better performance of PostgreSQL. To disable it:

Red Hat Enterprise Linux kernels:

```
# cat /sys/kernel/mm/redhat_transparent_hugepage/enabled
```

Other kernels:

```
# cat /sys/kernel/mm/transparent_hugepage/enabled
```

The following is a sample output that shows THP are being used as the [always] flag is enabled:

```
[always] never
```

Hugepages

Virtual memory is mapped to physical memory using a combination of software and hardware mechanisms. This virtual memory feature allows the OS to spread the addressable space into different areas of physical RAM.

But, this VM concept requires translation from virtual address to physical address. Information for this transformation is stored in "page tables." To speed up the lookup/translations in these tables, this table is stored in a cache called the Translation Lookaside Buffer (TLB)

The amount of memory that can be translated by this TLB cache is called "TLB reach." If there is a TLB miss, there is a bigger penalty associated.

As per x86 architecture, page size is 4K bytes. That means when a process uses 1GB of memory, that's 262144 entries to look up! The effect of this multiplies as memory size increases.

The idea of hugepage is to increase this 4K bytes to 2MB typically. That will dramatically reduce the number of page references.

The obvious performance gain is from fewer translations requiring fewer cycles. A less obvious benefit is that address translation information is typically stored in the L2 cache. Typically, database workloads get a 7% instant performance gain.

The biggest benefit of hugepages is more stable performance of database systems.

Summary

In this chapter, we talked about some initial steps after installation for developers and administrators, and also talked about all configuration files of PostgreSQL and recommendations on how to use them. We covered a few basic parameters that one should consider while setting up their environment initially. These recommendations include database parameters and OS parameters as well. In the next chapter, we will talk about user management and securing databases.

CHAPTER 3

User Management and Securing Databases

In the last chapter, we talked about configuring a PostgreSQL database for a better performance, which includes tuning of several database-related parameters based on their behavior and also about operating system-related parameters that help to improve performance. In this chapter, we are going to talk about user management in PostgreSQL and securing databases by managing user privileges. We will also cover different types of privileges at object level and how we can best plan to utilize those granular level privileges to secure the databases, and different types of encryption techniques that you can use to secure your data.

Before we talk about how to manage users and implement security, let us talk about what information we need to know for the setup. If you are working for a new implementation of a PostgreSQL environment or migrating from any enterprise database, you need to know basic information to start with. Let us go through a few questions, through which you will get a starting point.

© Baji Shaik 2020
B. Shaik, *PostgreSQL Configuration*, https://doi.org/10.1007/978-1-4842-5663-3_3

Information That You Need to Know

When you are discussing security implementation, here are some basic questions that you can ask your customer. Each of the following questions has a specific purpose, which helps you in creating a plan while implementing security on the PostgreSQL side.

Q1. What is your current user management?

Purpose: This is basic information that you need to know. Different customers have different user managements, like:

- One user per one application

- Multiple users per one application

- One user per multiple applications

Most of the time it is multiple users per application based on the user role. If a single user is used, it is difficult to maintain security. So, it is recommended to use multiple users and roles and assign privileges to roles based on the requirement.

Q2. How are users being created?

Purpose: You should know how the users are being created in the current environment or how they want users to be created. Some customers use tools to dynamically create users based on the requirement and remove those when they are done with the user's work. If that is the case, you might need to develop a script that can do that.

Q3.   Are you using different users for writing and reading the database?

Purpose: If the customer is using different users for reading and writing, you might need to create users according to the requirements. Basically, for writing, it could be a normal user with necessary permissions on objects that it can modify. However, for reading, you will need a read-only role, which can only read the required objects but not modify in any case. Sometimes, you need a read-only role for monitoring also. PostgreSQL 10 came up with few monitoring roles by default, which we will be covering in this chapter in the "Security Mechanisms" section.

Q4.   Do you have any password policy set up?

Purpose: Enterprise databases like Oracle and MS SQL server have password policies for users, like:

- PASSWORD_LIFE_TIME

- PASSWORD_REUSE_TIME

- PASSWORD_REUSE_MAX

- PASSWORD_VERIFY_FUNCTION

- PASSWORD_LOCK_TIME

- PASSWORD_GRACE_TIME

- INACTIVE_ACCOUNT_TIME

However, PostgreSQL has only PASSWORD_LIFE_TIME (basically, password expiration date) by default. No other functionality is available by default. However, you can use a password check module. More information is available at www.postgresql.org/docs/current/passwordcheck.html.

Q5.   Do you have row level security implemented?

Purpose: Check if the customer is currently using any row level security. If so, PostgreSQL also has an RLS (Row Level Security) feature available. If you get this information from the customer, you can prepare policies on PostgreSQL according to the requirement. We will be covering more about RLS in the "Security Mechanisms" section.

Q6.   Are you using SSL connectivity? If so, how are the certificates being managed?

Purpose: If the customer is using SSL connections (secure way to connect database), you need to enable this feature in PostgreSQL by turning on the ssl parameter in the configuration file. However, you need to know how they are managing the certificates. Are they self-managed or CA certified? That will enable the requirement of keeping the certificates on the PostgreSQL side.

Q7.   Do you have any auditing setup?

Purpose: Auditing is one of the key features that every modern database has and every customer tries to implement. Auditing can be a compliance requirement in many systems. If the system has to be equipped with auditing features, database level auditing can set at PostgreSQL as well. We will be covering more about this feature in the "Security Mechanisms" section.

Q8.   What is your current implementation of security?

Purpose: You need to know their current implementation of security so that you look for alternatives in PostgreSQL, as it has its own way of securing things. If they are using any external tools for securing the data, you might need to look for those functionalities in the available tools of PostgreSQL.

Q9.   What are your expectations with PostgreSQL toward security?

Purpose: This is very important. They cannot expect everything to be working in the same way as their source enterprise database (if they are migrating from an enterprise database). Every database has its own security mechanisms. They can be comparable; however, they might not match sometimes. So, you need to carefully evaluate their current security implementation and set the expectations accordingly when they are using PostgreSQL.

Q10.   Do you use encryption of data at rest or in motion? If so, how is it implemented?

Purpose: Encryption is another key aspect of security. It can be at rest or in motion. You need to know how it is implemented and come up with the tools that can give the same functionality in PostgreSQL. We will be covering more about encryption in the "Security Mechanisms" section.

Security Mechanisms

When a customer is migrating from an enterprise database (like Oracle or MS SQL server), they might want to know the basic level of security that PostgreSQL provides. You can distinguish security as different mechanisms, as follows:

- Authentication methods in HBA

- ACLs

- RLS—Row Level Security

- SSL/TLS connections

- Event triggers

- Auditing

- Monitoring roles

- Encryption and PCI

- Replication

- PL trusted vs. untrusted

The intent of this chapter is that after reading it, you will know what features PostgreSQL has in terms of user management and security. So if at any moment you encounter something, you may suddenly recall that PostgreSQL has RLS or there's something called event triggers that you could use for security purposes.

First things first: the PostgreSQL web site has a security page that contains information regarding all the common vulnerability information, and which minor versions of PostgreSQL and major versions are vulnerable and which aren't: `www.postgresql.org/support/security/`.

It is highly recommended to bookmark this page and check it out at least a few times a week by everyone who deals with PostgreSQL in their production environment. Security fixes take precedence over regular bugs. Security problems are identified and patched by the PostgreSQL community even more quickly. It's very useful.

Authentication in HBA

PostgreSQL basically authenticates connections to itself using an HBA file (Host Based Authentication file). If you install PostgreSQL and open a pg_hba.conf file, this file looks like the following by default:

```
# TYPE   DATABASE           USER          ADDRESS                    METHOD

# "local" is for Unix domain socket connections only
local    all                all                                      trust

# IPv4 local connections:
host     all                all           127.0.0.1/32               trust

# IPv6 local connections:
host     all                all           ::1/128                    trust

# Allow replication connections from localhost, by a user with the
# replication privilege.
local    replication        all                                      trust
host     replication        all           127.0.0.1/32               trust
host     replication        all           ::1/128                    trust
```

This is not ideally what it should look at once you have PostgreSQL running in production.

There are a lot of authentication types that PostgreSQL supports in its HBA. Different types of authentication methods are:

- PASSWORD

- MD5

- SCRAM

- TRUST

- REJECT

- PEER

- IDENT

- LDAP

- HOSTSSL

PASSWORD

This is the simplest password-based authentication system that PostgreSQL has. It is a plain text password. It is not encrypted and hence it is not ideal.

MD5

This is what is still in many ways the standard password authentication format and salted algorithm for hashing. It has some flaws that people criticize PostgreSQL for, like: "Why does PostgreSQL have md5? Isn't it broken?" However, the way PostgreSQL uses md5 is better than how base md5 would work. We actually have a random salt every time via authenticate that makes it a little bit more secure than what pure md5 would.

SCRAM

From PostgreSQL 10 onward, we have SCRAM (Salted Challenge Response Authentication Mechanism). SCRAM is better than md5, as it overcomes the flaws that md5 has. It is more secure; here is an example of setting up SCRAM password encryption in PostgreSQL 10:

```
postgres=# set password_encryption ='scram-sha-256';
SET
postgres=# CREATE ROLE finance WITH PASSWORD 'mostcommonpassword';
CREATE ROLE
```

```
postgres=# select substr(rolpassword,1,14) from pg_authid where
rolname ='finance';
     substr
----------------
 SCRAM-SHA-256$
(1 row)
postgres=#
```

And so, what's the difference when it comes to how SCRAM is better than md5 here? In the pg_authid table, if you have passwords encrypted in the md5 format, it is going to show you the md5 hash of it like the following:

```
postgres=# create role sales with password 'md5password';
CREATE ROLE
postgres=# select rolpassword from pg_authid where rolname
='sales';
              rolpassword
----------------------------------------
 md5059f18f30cad64836a01f936c9ba7dd4
(1 row)
```

It is not going to hide that information, so you can actually see the password hash, which is not ideal. It is much better than MySQL, which in its default format will store the password in plain text unless you wrap the password with a password function explicitly. PostgreSQL does not need you to wrap it in any function; if you give it a password it's automatically going to store it as a hashed value. However, with md5 the substring is a pure md5 hash, whereas you can see how SCRAM works in the previous example. So, SCRAM basically gives you the details of computing the value of the password. It does not give the hash, hence it is more secure. If you are thinking of upgrading to PostgreSQL 10 and possibly moving to SCRAM from md5 for a limited time at least for PostgreSQL 10 and 11, PostgreSQL is allowing fallback to md5. So, basically if you have your password encryption set to SCRAM and some client is trying to connect using md5 authentication, PostgreSQL is going to let that happen—just to ease the transition for people, but not in later versions.

An example entry in a pg_hba.conf file is as follows:

```
# All users (from 192.168.12.10) require SCRAM authentication
to connect postgres database.
```

```
# TYPE   DATABASE    USER    ADDRESS              METHOD
host     postgres    all     192.168.12.10/32     scram-sha-256
```

TRUST

Basically, "do not trust" the TRUST authentication. TRUST is basically no password at all. For example, "I'm just going to trust that you my best friend can do anything in my room you want to" and that leads to issues. One of the worst ways that this can happen is if you saw in the default file the very first line had TRUST authentication, so somebody who does not look into the documentation might just think "TRUST is simple and it is still authentication so I'm going to just use trust for all my other accesses as well." To eliminate that possibility there is a way in PostgreSQL: when you initialize the data directory, you can tell PostgreSQL not to put that line in the default HBA file. So, just remove it from the very root cause itself. That option is -A in initdb:

```
8c85902e3a2c:data $ initdb --help|grep auth
  -A, --auth=METHOD  default authentication method for local
        connections
      --auth-host=METHOD  default authentication method for
        local TCP/IP connections
      --auth-local=METHOD  default authentication method for
        local-socket connections
8c85902e3a2c:data $
```

It is the way to tell initdb to use md5 as the minimum level of authentication so there would be no trust if you generate a file using this option in a DB.

REJECT

Oftentimes you have a subset of IPs that you want to allow access for a particular role in a particular database; however, there might be one or two IPs within that subset that you do not want to allow access to. So, either you or one of your DBAs is lazy and they just think "nobody is going to access from those few IPs and I am just going to allow them all" or your DBA is nice where they just go the extra mile and don't put in the IP as a subnet but they put in individual IPS /32 even if there are a hundred. However, note that there is a reject option. What you can do is allow access to a subnet and set this particular IP reject, which means do not look at any line after this line. It is really important that you reject any superuser connecting from a host that is not the local host just for security purposes. Usually, if it is a DBA, they can SSH into the database server and log in as a superuser.

An example entry in pg_hba.conf file is as follows:

```
#All users from 192.168.54.1 server are rejected.
```

# TYPE	DATABASE	USER	ADDRESS	METHOD
host	all	all	192.168.54.1/32	reject

PEER and IDENT

In both these auth methods, PostgreSQL gets the OS user name from which the client is connecting and matches it with the requested database user name. The difference between these auth methods is that PEER is available for local connections whereas IDENT is for TCP/IP connections.

For peer auth, `pg_hba.conf` entry looks like the following:

```
# "local" is for Unix domain socket connections only
local    all          all                                    peer
```

For ident auth, `pg_hba.conf` entry looks like the following:

```
host    all    all    192.168.10.22/24    ident    map=my_ident_map
```

An `$PGDATA/ident.conf` file looks like the following:

```
# MAPNAME        SYSTEM-USERNAME        PG-USERNAME
my_ident_map       my_os_user           ident_db_user
```

LDAP

This auth method is used when your connection is being authenticated from an LDAP server.

Note   Any change that you make to an HBA file needs a reload of PostgreSQL server to take effect.

An example entry from `pg_hba.conf` looks like the following:

```
host    all    dbuser  0.0.0.0/0    ldap   ldapserver=ldapserver.
                                           example.com
                                           ldapprefix="cn="
                                           ldapsuffix=",
                                           dc=example, dc=com"
```

HOSTSSL

This auth method is used when you use SSL connections. Before you use this auth, you should turn on SSL parameters in the `postgresql.conf` configuration file.

An example entry looks like the following:

```
hostssl   all          all        0.0.0.0/0      md5
```

ACLs

ACL stands for Access Control List. So, basically this list shows a list of privileges that a user has on an object. These privileges are assigned by using the GRANT command and revoked by using the REVOKE command.

Available Privileges

Before we talk further, you need to know ACL privilege abbreviations as show in the following:

```
r — SELECT ("read")
w — UPDATE ("write")
a — INSERT ("append")
d — DELETE
D — TRUNCATE
x — REFERENCES
t — TRIGGER
X — EXECUTE
U — USAGE
C — CREATE
c — CONNECT
T — TEMPORARY
arwdDxt — ALL PRIVILEGES (for tables, varies for other objects)
* — grant option for preceding privilege
/yyyy — role that granted this privilege
```

These ACL abbreviations are well explained in the PostgreSQL documentation at `www.postgresql.org/docs/current/ddl-priv.html#PRIVILEGE-ABBREVS-TABLE`.

Every object type has different kinds of privileges that can be granted on them. This table explains about it: `www.postgresql.org/docs/current/ddl-priv.html#PRIVILEGES-SUMMARY-TABLE`.

So, based on the requirement, carefully GRANT/REVOKE privileges on the objects. In this way, you can secure a database to be against being accessed by unwanted users. When you compare it with other relational and enterprise databases, you are going to notice, aside from all the common ones (like SELECT, INSERT, DELETE, etc.), there is something called USAGE. This has a different meaning in PostgreSQL. This privilege lets user/role use a particular schema to access objects inside it for read/write purposes. Note that, though you have certain privileges on an object, unless you have usage on the schema in which the object exists, you cannot access the object. You can use \z to see the access privileges of an object. Here is an example:

```
postgres=# \z titles
                              Access privileges
 Schema |  Name  | Type  | Access privileges | Column privileges |
 Policies
--------+--------+-------+-------------------+-------------------+
----------
 public | titles | table |                   |                   |
(1 row)

postgres=# grant select,insert on titles to sales;
GRANT
Time: 27.145 ms
```

```
postgres=# \z titles
                              Access privileges
 Schema |  Name  | Type  |      Access privileges      |
 Column privileges | Policies
--------+--------+-------+-----------------------------+
------------------+----------
 public | titles | table | postgres=arwdDxt/postgres+|
                  |
        |        |       | sales=ar/postgres           |
                  |
(1 row)
```

Transactional DDLs

Unlike other database engines (like Oracle, MySQL, etc.), PostgreSQL has transaction DDLs. It means you can execute DDLs inside a transaction and commit/rollback if needed. Some relational databases allow you to run the DDLs inside a transaction but if you do a rollback, those do not really get rolled back. However, rollback of a DDL in a transaction really rolls it back in PostgreSQL. For example:

```
postgres=# begin;
BEGIN
postgres=# grant select on titles to sales;
GRANT
postgres=# \z titles
                              Access privileges
```

```
 Schema |  Name  | Type  |      Access privileges      |
 Column privileges | Policies
--------+--------+-------+-----------------------------+
-------------------+----------
 public | titles | table | postgres=arwdDxt/postgres+|
                          |
        |        |       | sales=r/postgres            |
                          |
(1 row)

postgres=# rollback;
ROLLBACK
postgres=# \z titles
                                Access privileges
 Schema |  Name  | Type  |      Access privileges      |
 Column privileges | Policies
--------+--------+-------+-----------------------------+
-------------------+----------
 public | titles | table | postgres=arwdDxt/postgres |
                          |
(1 row)
```

Alter Default Privileges

If you have a new schema and you know that all tables in that schema should have a set number of permissions by default, then you can give default privileges using some syntax similar to this:

```
ALTER DEFAULT PRIVILEGES IN SCHEMA <schema_name> GRANT
<privilege> ON TABLES TO <role>;
```

What happens even if your schema is empty? It will know that these are the default privileges for it, so the next step is to actually create a table within that schema; if you check the privileges using \dp, you'll see whatever permissions you wanted it to have. One thing to take note of is that you can set this on any schema even with existing objects in it After you execute alter default privileges and you create another object inside that schema, it is going to read these privileges and assign them automatically. However, it is not going to assign its default privileges to the objects that already exist inside the schema. You will have to do that manually. You can prepare commands or generate a SQL script.

Roles and Groups

The next thing about ACL is roles. Usually, roles and group roles are the norm, but PostgreSQL does not give any special kind of definition within itself to a group role. Any role can have other roles as its members. You don't have to have any special declaration for such a role. What you should do is by convention and good policy; you can have group roles like sales and have all the privileges that any person joining the sales team would require on a set of databases or a set of schemas. Any new person who joins the sales team will just have their own individual role and we just made them a member of the sales role, with no extra or special privileges for that particular salesperson. So, what happens that way is you have less work to do when that person leaves or even when a new person joins in. And that makes sure that there is no rogue permission for this particular user anywhere, and you drop it and suddenly the database is broken because that user doesn't exist anymore and they created the table.

Column Level ACLs

This is another very neat feature of PostgreSQL. You can have column level ACLs, as shown in the following:

```
postgres=# GRANT update(emp_no) ON titles TO sales;
GRANT
postgres=# \z titles
                                       Access privileges
 Schema |  Name  | Type  |      Access privileges      |
 Column privileges  | Policies
--------+--------+-------+-----------------------------+
--------------------+----------
 public | titles | table | postgres=arwdDxt/postgres |
 emp_no:           +|
        |        |       |                             |
   sales=w/postgres |
(1 row)

postgres=#
```

You can give column level privileges to users. The preceding example updates a particular column named emp_no to sales role and you can see that it has that privilege.

Avoid Public Schema

It is recommended that you should have your own schemas even though granting usage is a pain sometimes, especially if you're new to PostgreSQL, because the public schema by default allows access to everyone. So, it does not matter how important a function you create, if it's in the public schema, any user in your database can execute it. If you have one small application, you may think "Why do we need a separate schema? We might know exactly what roles are going to be there and we know exactly what permissions they're going to have." However, your being restrictive does not mean that PostgreSQL is going to be restrictive. By default, there is a public role that is assigned to a newly created role/user. You cannot really revoke the privileges from any users that are assigned through the public schema.

Read-Only Roles

A read-only role is one of the trickiest parts of PostgreSQL. As explained in the previous section, a `public` role will be assigned to a newly created user/role. So, by default the user/role gets privileges to create objects in the public schema. However, if you mean for a read-only role, it is supposed to read the objects from the database and should not have privilege to create the objects. But you cannot really revoke that permission from a user/role directly. However, you can revoke those privileges from a public role, which inherits all created users and new users going to be created.

```
#this will revoke create privileges from all the users
REVOKE CREATE ON SCHEMA public FROM public;
#you would need to explicitly grant privileges if you want a
user with write permissions
GRANT CREATE ON SCHEMA public to write;
#create read-only
CREATE ROLE user_readonly WITH PASSWORD 'mypassword';
GRANT SELECT ON ALL TABLES IN SCHEMA public TO user_readonly;
```

Note   if you revoke privileges from the `public` role, note that you will have to explicitly grant them to new users for whom you want to grant read/write access to the public schema.

RLS (Row Level Security)

RLS is all about restricting the access to a few rows of a table. It is introduced in PostgreSQL 9.5. You can say it is partial access of the table. Sometimes you may have a huge table (like accounts in the following example) in which you have data about managers and employees. You may have all sorts of sensitive information like salaries, and you might not want a manager to see the employee details of employees who are not reporting to him/her. So, in those cases either you can split the table into a thousand parts depending on how big your company is or you can make use of row level security. Some more important critical purposes arise if you go into government databases and you have more privacy issues, so for that purpose you can enable row level security. Here is an example:

```
postgres=# ALTER TABLE accounts ENABLE ROW LEVEL SECURITY;
ALTER TABLE
postgres=# CREATE POLICY account_managers ON accounts TO managers
postgres-# USING (manager = current_user);
CREATE POLICY
postgres=> \c - postgres
psql (11.2, server 10.2)
You are now connected to database "postgres" as user "postgres".
postgres=# select count(1) from accounts ;
 count
-------
     2
(1 row)

postgres=# \c - managers
psql (11.2, server 10.2)
You are now connected to database "postgres" as user "managers".
postgres=> select * from accounts ;
```

```
 manager  | employee | contact_email | salary
----------+----------+---------------+--------
 managers | employee | abc@abc.com   | 100000
(1 row)
postgres=> select count(1) from accounts ;
 count
-------
     1
(1 row)
```

So, basically in the preceding example, it is creating a policy that states that if your current user is listed as a manager in a subset of the rows in the accounts table, this user can only see those specific rows. This is a very simple policy but that's the way it works. Even if this current user "selects * from accounts", they can only see the rows for which they are manager. There are exceptions and you can grant exceptions. So, say, abc user is the top level manager of the organization but you don't want him to be the owner of the table. He has a regular, non-superuser account in PostgreSQL, but he needs to see the whole table; you can provide him bypass RLS privilege as shown in the following:

ALTER ROLE abc BYPASSRLS;

The table owner is automatically exempted from the restriction of RLS. If you own the table, even though you have row level enabled you will be able to see all the rows. If you want that to happen, you have to do a force keyword when you're defining row level enabling.

ALTER TABLE accounts FORCE ROW LEVEL SECURITY;

> **Note**   The default policy when you enable row level is all denied
> so unless you create a policy, nobody can select anything from that
> table. So, if you are planning to enable it, make sure you do both of
> these things (enabling and creating policy) in a single transaction.

In PostgreSQL 9.5 and 9.6, if you have three policies on the table
and you're trying to query something, then the user need not satisfy all
three policies. If the user can get through any one of those policies, that
is sufficient to get access. This was the only option you had when you
had multiple policies—only the OR logic. However, from PostgreSQL 10
onward, you also have AND or restrictive, wherein if a user cannot get
through all of these policies, they cannot read anything from the table.

SSL

As you know, SSL is one of the secure ways to connect a database. If you
want to make SSL connections, you should turn on SSL, which will require
a restart. If you're installing or compiling your own PostgreSQL, make sure
you compile it with open SSL like the following:

```
./configure --with-openssl
```

By default, SSL will allow for both authentication and encryption. You
can choose not to encrypt. Some people feel like it's too much overhead,
but you have the option. But just because you have the option doesn't
mean you should use it, because most of the workload in SSL goes into the
authentication and encryption, which doesn't take much time or resource
consumption. So, if you are already decided to use SSL, why not just
encrypt it too.

Here are certificates you need and parameters to set the certificate locations:

```
ssl = on # (change requires restart)
#ssl_ciphers = 'ALL:!ADH:!LOW:!EXP:!MD5:@STRENGTH' # allowed
SSL ciphers #ssl_prefer_server_ciphers = on # (change requires
restart) #ssl_ecdh_curve = 'prime256v1' # (change requires
restart)
ssl_cert_file = '/etc/ssl/postgres/starry.io.crt' # (change
requires restart)
ssl_key_file = '/etc/ssl/postgres/starry.io.key' # (change
requires restart) ssl_ca_file = " # (change requires restart)
#ssl_crl_file = " # (change requires restart)
```

Make sure the certificate permissions are 600, otherwise PostgreSQL will refuse to start.

Until Postgres 9.6, whenever you had to change your certificate you required a restart. However, you just need a reload from PostgreSQL 10.

Tunneling

If you have SSL supported and you want all connections from SSL but you have an outdated client that does not support SSL, there is always SSH tunneling and you can still have SSL enabled

```
ssh -L 63333:localhost:5432 foo@bar.com
psql -h localhost -p 63333 postgres
```

Event Trigger

The way event triggers differ from normal triggers is that these don't fire on DDLs at all. They fire on bigger events like you have a new DBA and it's their first day on the job and they drop the users table. Event triggers are going to prevent that. It is not something that will get used every day, but it's the one thing that will save you and your web site. On the one day that somebody makes a major mistake, an event trigger is going to save you. So, basically the advantages of event triggers are:

- Auditing

- Unwanted modification of data

- Accidental data loss

Let us look at an example:

```
postgres=# CREATE FUNCTION to_avoid_object_drops()
postgres-#          RETURNS event_trigger
postgres-# LANGUAGE plpgsql AS $$
postgres$# DECLARE
postgres$#     object record;
postgres$# BEGIN
postgres$#     FOR object IN SELECT * FROM pg_event_trigger_
               dropped_objects()
postgres$#     LOOP
postgres$#         RAISE EXCEPTION '% dropped object: % %.% %',
postgres$#                         tg_tag,
postgres$#                         object.object_type,
postgres$#                         object.schema_name,
postgres$#                         object.object_name,
postgres$#                         object.object_identity;
postgres$#     END LOOP;
postgres$# END
```

```
postgres$# $$;
CREATE FUNCTION

postgres=# CREATE EVENT TRIGGER to_avoid_object_drops
postgres-#    ON sql_drop
postgres-#    EXECUTE PROCEDURE to_avoid_object_drops();
CREATE EVENT TRIGGER

postgres=# DROP TABLE join1;
NOTICE:  DROP TABLE dropped object: table public.join1 public.
         join1
NOTICE:  DROP TABLE dropped object: index public.unq_index_join
         public.unq_index_join
NOTICE:  DROP TABLE dropped object: type public.join1 public.
         join1
NOTICE:  DROP TABLE dropped object: type public._join1 public.
         join1[]
NOTICE:  DROP TABLE dropped object: toast table pg_toast.pg_
         toast_16554 pg_toast.pg_toast_16554
NOTICE:  DROP TABLE dropped object: index pg_toast.pg_
         toast_16554_index pg_toast.pg_toast_16554_index
NOTICE:  DROP TABLE dropped object: type pg_toast.pg_
         toast_16554 pg_toast.pg_toast_16554
ERROR:   DROP TABLE dropped object: table public.join1 public.
         join1
CONTEXT: PL/pgSQL function to_avoid_object_drops() line 7 at RAISE
```

These are the four events that as of right now event triggers support:

- ddl_command_start

- ddl_command_end

- sql_drop

- table_rewrite in pg10

In our previous example, it was an SQL drop event. `ddl_command_start` and `ddl_command_end` are equivalent to normal triggers before and after a DDL command. As for table rewrites, some activities like altering a columns data type or setting a default value to a column is not the best thing to do when it is peak load time for your web site. You can prevent that from happening by creating an event trigger that checks for a table rewrite operation and you can disallow that sort of operation when it is a bad time. So, you can say that you can only do these operations from 12 a.m. to 9 a.m.

Auditing

PostgreSQL does not have a core auditing extension, so you can create a normal DML trigger and just get the difference of the new values and the old values and store it in another table. Here is a simple example:

```
CREATE FUNCTION test_audit_trig() RETURNS trigger
        LANGUAGE plpgsql
        AS $$
DECLARE
        v_dmltype    text;
BEGIN
IF TG_OP = 'INSERT' THEN
    v_dmltype = 'I';
ELSE
    v_dmltype = 'U';
END IF;

INSERT INTO auditing.test (col1, col2,....dmltype,
change_timestamp)
VALUES (NEW.col1, NEW.col2,....v_dmltype, current_timestamp)
RETURN NULL;
```

Attach trigger to a table:

```
CREATE TRIGGER test_audit_trig BEFORE INSERT OR UPDATE OR
DELETE ON table_name
    FOR EACH ROW EXECUTE PROCEDURE test_audit_trig();
```

pgaudit is the closest that PostgreSQL has when it comes to an auditing extension. However, keep in mind that it is not a core PostgreSQL extension. The pgaudit extension is useful if your whole database needs to be audited.

Monitoring Roles

PostgreSQL 10 onward, when it comes to monitoring there are new monitoring roles. Before PostgreSQL 10, if you wanted to connect a monitoring tool with your instance, the user that tool used to talk to PostgreSQL had to be a superuser because there are things in your catalog metadata information that a non-superuser cannot query. So, if you wanted certain types of information you had to have a superuser. However, PostgreSQL 10 onward there are new monitoring roles available:

- pg_monitor
- pg_read_all_settings
- pg_read_all_stats
- pg_stat_scan_tables

Encryption and PCI

pgcrypto is used to achieve database level encryption in PostgreSQL. It is a PostgreSQL core extension and not a third-party tool. It is still an extension, but it is supported by the PostgreSQL community so it is trustworthy. Now, what should be encrypted when we talk about encryption? Let's talk about:

- Performance impact

- Backups

- Volumes

- Instance level

Performance Impact

You can have different types of AES algorithms (like AES-128, AES-192, or AES-256) in pgcrypto. There is going to be an obvious performance impact. So, basically you are telling pgcrypto to encrypt each atomic value in your table or set of tables. You can choose to either encrypt the whole table or encrypt only the important columns that you want to protect. When it comes to PCI and credit card data (for example), you have one of the columns in your credit card table and that is the credit card number, for example; that is the only one that you really need to protect depending on what other columns you have. However, you certainly don't need to encrypt the whole table because you have information in there that by itself is not going to be useful to a bad party. Here is an example on using pgcrypto functions:

```
postgres=# CREATE TABLE crypt_table(uname varchar, pwd_crypt
text, pwd_md5 text);
CREATE TABLE
```

```
postgres=# create extension pgcrypto ;
CREATE EXTENSION
postgres=# INSERT INTO crypt_table VALUES ('Robert',
crypt('testpassword',gen_salt('md5')),md5('testpassword'));
INSERT 0 1
postgres=# INSERT INTO crypt_table VALUES ('Tom',
crypt('testpassword',gen_salt('md5')),md5('testpassword'));
INSERT 0 1
postgres=# select * from crypt_table ;
 uname  |              pwd_crypt              |
            pwd_md5
--------+------------------------------------+
----------------------------------
 Robert | $1$Y3iUMA6h$OUTGwuH7hoFJnOO48taNV1 |
 e16b2ab8d12314bf4efbd6203906ea6c
 Tom    | $1$IfATTihP$A78rkOIIEvkZ2LjcRT6hd1 |
 e16b2ab8d12314bf4efbd6203906ea6c
(2 rows)
postgres=# select uname from crypt_table where uname='Tom' and
pwd_crypt=crypt('testpassword',pwd_crypt);
 uname
-------
 Tom
(1 row)
```

Backups

Backups should be encrypted. One key requirement about PCI is that you do not want to have the encryption keys with your backup because if your backup is stolen, the key goes with it. There goes all the data, so it's preferable to use pg_dump because that way you can just take a logical backup. Your filesystem won't get backed up and hence your keys.

Volumes

There is also an option with certain filesystems to encrypt. You can have an encrypted back volume on ZFS (for example) and you can do all sorts of secure things like require a split key start. So, you cannot even restore or bring the volume up unless two people put in their own specific passwords.

Instance Level

What about instance level encryption on a running instance? There is growing demand for data at rest encryption—TDE (Transparent Data Encryption). However, there is nothing in PostgreSQL yet. There is a proof-of-concept patch being discussed here: `www.postgresql.org/message-id/ flat/CA%2BCSw_tb3bk5i7if6inZFc3yyf%2B9HEVNTy51QFBoeUk7UE_V%3Dw %40mail.gmail.com`. There are multiple efforts like this in the community, but they are not completed yet.

Replication

Why would replication be discussed as a part of security? Sometimes, especially when it's a PCI environment and you need to take care of a credit card database, it is recommended to not have a hot standby. Because, if you have a read-only replica, anybody can select and read anything on your replica without getting trapped. If you have a PCI replica, you have to be extremely sure that outside of that nobody can access it, because even the DBA shouldn't be able to.

If you have a recovery file—which you should if you have a replica—try not to have the plain text password in the connection string in your recovery file. The simplest way to avoid that is to have a .pgpass file. It is a secret file in the PostgreSQL home directory and it is a dot file with very restricted permission 600. It will allow you to connect without having to explicitly write down your password or have it in plain text in your recovery conf.

PL Trusted vs. Untrusted

Procedures untrusted are basically those that can access and manipulate things outside the database, and trusted are those that are only allowed to manipulate and do things inside the database management software.

If you want a nonprivileged user to have an escalated privilege for the purpose of executing a particular function, you can use a "security definer" keyword in the function that you're creating. Basically, what security definer does is that when a user tries to run a function, it gives the user elevated privileges to be able to run that function as an owner of the function. So, it's quite useful if you just want a user to run a specific function but do not want them to have that privilege all the time.

High Security and Encryption Guidelines

- Never open port 5432 to the public Internet.

- Do not give permissions to any user to SSH to the database server. Rather, use a bastion host and open port for that host.

- If you plan for bastion host, restrict access with VPN.

- If you are on cloud-based managed services, make sure you have the right security groups (open to necessary hosts).

- Make sure you always update your database with the latest security patches. Security patches information is here: `www.postgresql.org/support/security/`.

- Never, ever use the "trust" auth method in pg_hba.conf.

- Always create "roles" with necessary grants and assign right roles to right users.

- While encrypting the data, consider encrypting only required columns but not all tables or the whole database.

- Do not log sensitive information in cleartext.

- Make sure you encrypt backups.

- Restrict access of users to required rows using RLS.

- Try doing encryption at the application side, not on the database.

Summary

In this chapter, we have talked about object level privileges in PostgreSQL and how to use them to secure your database. Creating roles and separating them based on the usage from application gives you better security over your data. Depending on the data sensitivity, you can encrypt your data using available PostgreSQL extensions like pgcrypto. We have also talked about a few guidelines that you can consider before you implement your database security. In the next chapter, we will talk about backup/restore options available and how to build a backup strategy of your database, depending on the information available from the customer.

CHAPTER 4

Backup and Restore Best Practices

In the last chapter, we talked about user management in PostgreSQL using roles by assigning proper privileges and secure data by encrypting using the pgcrypto module. It helps to improve security by controlling object and data access. In this chapter, we are going to talk about backup/ restore strategies and procedures. Building these strategies needs a lot of information. This chapter walks you through the stages in which information will be gathered to set up backup/restore for a database, based on the criticality of the data. This chapter also talks about when to/what to/ how to backup/restore.

Purpose of Backing Up a Database

It is actually surprising how often these days, as a consultant going out to different customers, you run into this scenario: they don't have backups and you hear things like "Well, you know, we have replication. We don't really need to do backups because our replication will take care of that." That's not really how it works. When you drop the wrong table, that replicates instantly to the replica and there is never any chance to stop that before it's too late. In earlier days, backups were needed for disaster recoveries (which meant bringing up the whole database in case of failures). However, there are a lot of procedures to save databases from disaster recoveries nowadays (which we will be discussing in Chapter 7).

© Baji Shaik 2020
B. Shaik, *PostgreSQL Configuration*, https://doi.org/10.1007/978-1-4842-5663-3_4

You might have heard of customers saying they are running in the cloud so they don't need backups. You possibly need backups more than ever if you do that now; you might have somebody else take the backups for you as part of your service agreement, but there needs to be backups. A few customers may say that they run their things on Docker, so they don't need to take separate backups. It is strongly recommended to take the backups in either of the cases.

The main purpose of backup is point-in-time-recovery (PITR), which means restoring the database to a point in time. PITR is needed when any accidental changes happen in the database and those have to be corrected or restored back in the database to continue business.

Gather Information to Set Up a Backup Strategy

There are a lot of questions that need to be answered to plan backup. Once you gather all the information, you can plan a backup strategy. Let us look at some questions:

Q1. What is the criticality of the data?

Purpose: You need to know how critical data is before setting up a backup strategy. Depending on criticality, you plan on how frequently you take backup, what should be the retention, and how fast you can recover the data if needed.

Q2. How sensitive is the data?

Purpose: If the data is too sensitive, you should plan for encryption of backups. As encryption might be overhead, you should know if the backups need to be encrypted or not.

Q3.   How much downtime can you afford in case PITR is needed?

Purpose: You should know how much downtime you can afford in worst-case scenarios. Depending on this information, you would know how frequently you need to back up your database. You always choose a worst-case scenario to calculate the affordable downtime.

Q4.   How big is the database?

Purpose: Depending on database size, you would plan for backup servers and retentions, and also decide what kind of backup you can choose for your database.

Q5.   Would you be able to afford cloud storage or a physical/virtual server for backups?

Purpose: It is always recommended to store your backups on a different machine than the database machine. So, you should ask this question of the customer before you implement a backup strategy.

Q6.   What will be the retention of backups?

Purpose: To plan storage for the backups, you need to know the retention. Customer should know how many backups they would need in case of failures.

Q7.   How much maintenance window can be provided for taking backups?

Purpose: Depending on the maintenance window of backups, you can plan on backup frequency and kind of backups.

Q8.   What kind of backup do you want?

Purpose: Some customers might be specific about what kind of backups they want. However, if the customer requests, you need to recommend what kind of backups they can go for, based on the information you gather.

Backup Types

When talking about database backups, what about backups in PostgreSQL? There are two fundamentally different approaches to backing up PostgreSQL databases:

- Logical backups

- Physical backups

Logical Backups

Logical backups are also known as SQL dumps. PostgreSQL has "pg_dump" through which you can take a logical backup. Here are a few options using pg_dump:

As "pg_dump" is one of the most commonly known methods for backing up of PostgreSQL and easy to use, people might decide to use it for their backup solution. It lets you do some nice things like using a custom format—you can do compression in parallel, do data only or schema only, and pick exactly which things you want. So, pg_dump is awesome in a lot of ways, but it has some limitations:

- Too slow to restore

- Too much overhead

- No PITR

However, nowadays, pg_dump really is not a backup solution. It has many use cases but backup is not one of them unless your database is really small (less than a couple of GB). Even if your database is really small, it probably is not the right solution anyway due to limitations explained previously.

Using pg_dump is very simple but it usually takes too long to do the backup. That is usually OK, but the real problem is it takes too long to restore because pg_dump will recreate your tables and then rebuild all your indexes. So, if you're using a pg-dump based backup for some reason, make sure that you actually test it over time to see how long your restore time is going to be. There is just too much overhead, and even on small databases the problem is you cannot do PITR.

For more details on pg_dump and pg_dumpall, please go through: www.postgresql.org/docs/current/app-pgdump.html and www.postgresql.org/docs/current/app-pg-dumpall.html.

How to Take Logical Backups

Let us see some examples here:

- To take the dump of a whole cluster:

  pg_dumpall -p port > $backup_location/dumpall.sql

  Where -p is port of cluster.

- To take the dump of a database (use pg_dump for that)

  Plain format:

  pg_dump -p port -U user_name db_name > $backup_location/dump_postgres_db.sql

  Compressed format:

  pg_dump -p port -U user_name dbname -Fc -f $backup_location/dump.dmp

```
Where  -p – port
             -U – user
             -Fc – Format compressed (you can use tar by
                   using -Ft)
             -f – dumpfile.
```

- To take the dump of a table/sequence:

```
pg_dump -p port -U user_name -t table_name db_name >
$backup_location/dump_test_table.sql

    Where -t - tablename/sequencename
```

Physical Backups

If you are planning for backups, you should be looking at doing physical backups. These backups are called base backups:

- Fast restore

- Full cluster only

- Platform specific

The biggest advantages of physical backup are it is fast to restore and you can do PITR. You can only back up everything. You cannot back up an individual database or an individual table or schema. It is platform specific. You can take a dump or a backup on a 64-bit system and restore it on a 32-bit. But you can't switch from 32-bit to 64-bit.

How to Take a Base Backup

Let us start with a sample script that a lot of people use to take a base backup:

```
#!/bin/bash
set -e
psql -U postgres -q "SELECT pg_start_backup('foo')" # 'foo' is
a label which identifies this backup.
tar cfz /backup/$(date +%Y%m%d).tar.gz /var/lib/pgsql/data
psql -U postgres -q "SELECT pg_stop_backup()"
```

This is a traditional procedure that is used to take the backup. So, it starts the backup by using the pg_start_backup function, then copies the data directory to a backup location, and then stops backup using the pg_stop_backup function. However, the most common mistake is the error check. When the tar command fails at some point:

- It will abort, leaving your system in backup mode, and you will not be able to take another backup.

- You really do not want your system to crash now, because it's left things (backup_label file) around in the data directory that will make your system unable to start if it crashed.

There are so many ways to get this wrong; this used to be the only way, but there are many scripts out there that people use that do this.

To overcome this, PostgreSQL provides the pg_basebackup tool, which basically takes these base backups in the same way as the traditional procedure but instead of you running commands, it runs just as a PostgreSQL client.

If you need a simple PostgreSQL backup without making any setups and don't want to add a lot of complexity, then use the pg_basebackup tool. Also, if you're doing pg_dump for your backup solutions, you should really look at just switching to pg_basebackup. Here is a simple script:

```
#!/bin/bash
set -e
pg_basebackup -D /backup/$(date +%Y%m%d) -Ft -X fetch
```

-X includes required WALs in the backup. "fetch" indicates that WALs are collected at the end of the backup.

You just need to give a directory to copy backup files and indicate which format you want.

However, to make this work you need to have replication enabled in the hba file. You should have a line like this:

```
local replication postgres peer
```

And the following parameters in postgresql.conf file:

```
wal_level = hot_standby
max_wal_senders = 10
```

If you are on PostgreSQL 10 or older, you would need to set the preceding parameters. Otherwise, newer than 10, default value of wal_level is replica and max_wal_senders is 10. "max_wal_senders" is the same as max connections, just for replication connections.

Backup Formats

pg_basebackup can write your backups in two different formats:

- plain
  - Safe copy of data directory
  - Not good with multiple tablespaces
- tar
  - Destination still a directory
  - Each tablespace gets one file

It can use plain format, in which case basically your backup will be a copy that looks exactly like your data directory with all the subdirectories and all the files. However, it's done in a safe way so it will actually be a consistent data directory in the end, together with the transaction log.

Plain works well if you have one tablespace. If you have multiple tablespaces, by default it will have to write all the tablespace in the same location that they already are, which obviously only works if you're doing this across the network. In recent versions you can remap your tablespaces to different locations, but it rapidly becomes very complicated to use the plain format if you have multiple tablespaces. The other format for pg_basebackup is tar, in which case the destination is still a directory and you will put tar files into that directory. Your root tablespace will be in a file called base.tar or, if you're doing compression it will be base.tar.gz and then there will be one tar file for each tablespace. So, in a lot of ways that's easier for dealing with scenarios where you have more than one tablespace.

Always use -x or -X (using -x is equivalent to -X fetch) to include WAL files in the backup. You can use the following command:

```
$ pg_basebackup -x -D /path/to/backupdir
```

pg_basebackup can also support compressed backups. It uses standard gzip compression. You can use the "-Z" option for that. One thing to remember is if you use -Z, the compression is done by pg_basebackup and not by PostgreSQL. So, if you run pg-basebackup across the network to PostgreSQL, the data will be sent uncompressed from PostgreSQL to pg_basebackup and then compressed and written to disk

---

Note   Compression is only supported for the tar format and compression is CPU bound.

What Needs to Be Backed Up?

In order to actually use a base backup, what do you need?

You need all the transaction logs (WALs) generated on your system from the beginning of the backup to the end of the backup. PostgreSQL basically takes an inconsistent copy of your data directory and then it uses the transaction log to make it consistent. So, if you do not have the transaction log, it is not a consistent backup, which means you don't have a valid backup.

pg_receivexlog/pg_receivewal

One recommended way to set WAL backup is using the built-in PostgreSQL tool called pg_receivexlog (which is pg_receivewal from PostgreSQL 10). It is very easier to set up than your archive_command. You can run it on your archive server, but do not archive to the same machine that your database is on. If you lose the primary machine, you will lose both your backups and your primaries.

If you run pg_receivexlog, it connects to PostgreSQL over the replication protocol. It's basically a PostgreSQL replication standby without PostgreSQL, and it regenerates the log archive based on the replication data on your archive server. It gives you a more granular recovery. With an archive command, data gets sent in blocks of 16 megabytes; but with pg_receivexlog, they get sent in chunks, as it uses streaming protocol to stream the WALs. Hence, it doesn't need to wait for the WAL segment to get completed. It is safe against server restarts. If your server reboots in the middle of running your archived command—like your cp command is running but it didn't finish and then the server rebooted—then data loss or data corruption can happen. pg_receivexlog can take care of that, as it can follow timeline switches on the master.

Always use pg_receivexlog together with a replication slot so that no xlog will be removed before they back up. The replication slot ensures that no WAL is removed from primary until they have been received by all standbys. More information is available at: `www.postgresql.org/docs/current/warm-standby.html#STREAMING-REPLICATION-SLOTS`.

```
pg_receivewal -D /log/archive -h master -S backup
```

```
-S is for replication slot.
```

Backup Retention

The next question that people end up asking after the backup setup is "What about backup retention? How long am I going to keep my backups?" The best way to get answers to these questions is to contact the customer. If they want 10 years retention, that is fine but it needs lot of space, and if they want restore it will take a lot of time. If customers can come up with a strategy on how far they might need to go back for any situation, then you can set up retention based on it. Once that is decided, here is a sample script to remove your backups based on retention:

```
#!/bin/bash
find /var/backups/basebackup -type f -mtime +30 -print0 | xargs
-0 -r /bin/rm
find /var/backups/wal -type f -mtime +7 -print0 | xargs -0 -r /
bin/rm
```

So, in this example, we are deleting all our base backups older than 30 days. Sometimes, maybe that is not the best thing. You might want to keep some backups older than that in your staging server or copy them to tape. And then we are saying delete all the transaction log in the archive older than 7 days. So, that means going back one week, you can restore using PITR to an individual transaction or microsecond level. Beyond that, you can restore with the granularity of 1 day up to 30 days; once you've reached that point, you can't restore anymore.

Other Backup Tools

There are a couple of tools a little bit more advanced than what pg_basebackup can do. Those are:

- pgBackRest
- Barman

Barman

The Barman tool is developed by the 2ndQuadrant company and written in Python. Features of this tool are:

- Backup scheduling
- Log archiving
- Retention management
- Multiserver
- Restore shortcuts

It is gplv3 licensed. You can download from here: `https://github.com/2ndquadrant-it/barman`. Documentation is available here: `http://docs.pgbarman.org/release/2.9/`.

It primarily uses SSH and rsync to transfer both base backups and transaction logs. It is pretty simple to set up. You can go through documentation to set it up. However, you need to come up with a backup strategy before you set it up.

pgBackRest

pgBackRest is another open source tool to set up backups. It is built by the CrunchyData company and written in Perl. Features of this tool are:

- Backup scheduling

- Log archiving

- Retention management

- Multiserver

- Restore shortcuts

- Obsessive validation

That's a fairly similar list of features when compared with Barman. These tools solve the same problem, so the feature list is similar. However, once you get into the details, the implementations are different. Documentation is available here: https://pgbackrest.org/.

It's MIT licensed. It uses SSH but it doesn't use rsync. It uses its own protocol tunneled over SSH. The protocol is the enabler of the features that pgBackRest has that Barman doesn't. In particular, it supports parallel backup sessions so you can scale out and make your backups run faster. For most people, single threaded backups are not really a problem. But if your database is big, being able to do multithreaded backups can save your backup time significantly and also obviously your restore time when you're getting things back, which is more important.

It also supports full differential and incremental backups, and it does this at a segment basis. In PostgreSQL, we have all our tables split into segments of one gigabyte, and backrest basically functions like "if nothing in that one gigabyte has been modified, then I don't need to back it up again. If even a single byte has been modified, I'll copy the whole segment." Because if you actually want to look at every block, it'll just take too long to figure out if something has changed. Doing it at a gigabyte means if large portions of your database are read-only, your backups will be much faster because we can just skip that and get it from the previous full or differential backups.

It does not support concurrent backups

Restore Your Database

Until now, we have talked about backup types. Let us look at restoring database backups (logical and physical).

Logical Backups

There are two ways to restore a PostgreSQL database:

- psql for restoring from a plain SQL script file created with pg_dump

- pg_restore for restoring from a .tar file, directory, or custom format created with pg_dump

Restoring a Plain Dump File

It is pretty simple to restore a plain dump file generated by pg_dump. You can just use the "psql" utility for that. The following is an example:

```
psql -d db -U user -p port -h host -f dump_file.sql
```

Restoring Custom/tar Format Dump Files

You can use pg_restore to restore custom/tar format dump files. The following is an example:

```
# restoring a custom format file
$ pg_restore -U db_user -d db_name_new -v -1 db_name.dmp

# restore a single table from the dump
$ pg_restore -U db_user -d db_name_new --table=mytable -v -1
db_name.dmp

# restore a single function from the dump
$ pg_restore -U db_user -d db_name_new --function=myfunc -v -1
db_name.dmp
```

where db_user is the database user, db_name is the target database name, and db_name.dmp is the name of your backup file.

If you use pg_restore, you have various options available, for example:

-c to drop database objects before recreating them

-C to create a database before restoring into it

-e exit if an error has encountered

-F format to specify the format of the archive

Use "pg_restore -?" to get the full list of available options.

Restore Physical Backups

If it is offline backup that was taken when the database was down, then restore is pretty straightforward. You can just copy the backup directory to the location where you want your new restore database to run, and unzip and start the instance using pg_ctl.

```
$ pg_ctl stop postgresql
$ sudo rm -rf /path/to/data/directory/*
$ tar -xvC /path/to/data/directory -f /path/to/dumpdir/base.tar.gz
$ pg_ctl start postgresql
```

Point-In-Time-Recovery

To do a PITR, you need a full backup and WALs generated to the point of recovery you want. You just have to copy all your archives to some location and create a recovery.conf file in a restored data directory location.

```
restore_command = 'cp /tmp/demo/archive/%f "%p"'
recovery_target_time = '2019-08-31 15:00:00'
```

The restore_command specifies how to fetch a WAL file required by PostgreSQL. It is the inverse of archive_command. The recovery_target_time specifies the time until we need the changes.

All available recovery settings are here: `www.postgresql.org/docs/11/recovery-target-settings.html`.

Once the recovery.conf file is ready with the preceding contents, you can start the server using pg_ctl.

```
pg_ctl -D /restored/data/directory start
```

If it has to apply archive files on top of backup for recovery, you would see messages like the following in the log file:

```
LOG:  restored log file "000000010000000300000022" from archive
LOG:  restored log file "000000010000000300000023" from archive
LOG:  restored log file "000000010000000300000024" from archive
```

Once recovery is completed, you can see the following messages:

```
LOG: consistent recovery state reached at 0/40156B0
LOG: database system is ready to accept read only connections
```

You can now use the recovered database.

Design a Backup Strategy

Now it's time to set up a backup strategy based on the information from the earlier "Gather Information to Set Up a Backup Strategy" section. You can design backups as:

- Daily backups

- Weekly backups

- Monthly backups

- Yearly backups

You can find a few backup scripts to schedule automated backups here: `https://wiki.postgresql.org/wiki/Automated_Backup_on_Linux`.

Daily Backups

Based on the information gathered, there might be some databases that need backup every day. Typically, databases with the following behavior might need a daily backup:

- Databases that hold users' login (of a web site) information

- Critical databases with small size

Weekly Backups

Medium-sized databases will fall under this category. This is a very common type of backup that an administrator prefers.

Monthly Backups

If you have a backup retention of a few months, then it is recommended to have a monthly backup policy as well. This way, you can avoid restoring of weekly backup, which will reduce the restoration time.

Yearly Backup

Very few databases need a yearly backup policy. If you have a backup retention of multiple years, then it is recommended. These kinds of databases might hold historical data and are mostly used for archival purposes.

Monitoring Backups

It is not sufficient to just add cron jobs for backup; you need to monitor them too!

Be sure to monitor:

- Whether your backup jobs are completing successfully

- The time taken for each backup, and keep an eye on how this goes up

Additionally, you should also have another cron job that picks up a recent backup, tries to restore it into an empty database, and then deletes the database. This ensures that your backups are accessible and usable. Make sure you try restoring against the right versions of your PostgreSQL server.

You should monitor this restoration cron job too, as well as the time taken for the restoration. The restoration time has a direct impact on how long it'll be before you are back online after a database crash.

Summary

In this chapter, we have talked about what information you need to set up a backup strategy and how to set up a backup policy once you get the required information. We have also covered types of backups (physical and logical), how to take a backup, and how to restore the backups. Monitoring backup is also important, as discussed. In the next chapter, we will talk about the importance of logging database activities and best practices for enabling logging. We will also talk about monitoring the databases using database queries and external tools.

CHAPTER 5

Enable Logging of Your Database and Monitoring PostgreSQL Instances

In the last chapter, we talked about the stages in which information can be gathered to set up backup/restore for a database. We also talked about the types of backup and how to restore them when required. We walked through how you can set up a backup strategy for your data. In this chapter, we will talk about the importance of logging your database and what parameters should be considered as part of logging. We will also talk about when to log and how to use the information logged. We will go through how important monitoring of a database is and what factors should be considered while monitoring it. We will also cover a few monitoring tools available on the market.

Why/When/How to Log

Let us start with why logging is so important. You may be wondering why you even want logs. There could be many reasons to enable logging:

© Baji Shaik 2020

B. Shaik, *PostgreSQL Configuration*, https://doi.org/10.1007/978-1-4842-5663-3_5

- Maybe you want to know when your database was restarted. Somebody did this and you were not aware of it.

- Dropped an object or updated/deleted some data

- Detecting inefficient queries

It is always fun and challenge to know about these things when they happen and a great way to find out about that is in your PostgreSQL activity log.

Logging has upsides and downsides. The upside is that you get lots of information, which helps you in debugging the issues. The downside is that logging can actually slow your system down so that's something to be aware of and to consider.

Parameters to Set for Logging

There are a lot of different parameters in the PostgreSQL configuration file (postgresql.conf), and the following are some important parameters that need to be considered to set logging:

- log_min_duration_statement

- log_line_prefix

- log_checkpoints

- log_connections

- log_disconnections

- log_lock_waits

- log_temp_files

- log_autovacuum_min_duration

Note   The logging_collector parameter should be enabled to log anything in the database log files.

---

log_min_duration_statement

This parameter causes each statement that ran for at least the specified number of milliseconds to be logged. However, setting this parameter to a lower value causes more statements to be logged, potentially resulting in very large log files and increasing the amount of write activity on the server. The main advantage of configuring this parameter is identifying slow queries that would require optimization, and it is usually set at a value above which queries would be considered unacceptably slow.

This parameter is what really allows you to get the information that you need in the log file for something like pgBadger (it is a log analysis tool that gives you detailed reports and graphs) or even some of the other tools. These tools enable you to analyze those queries and roll them up, and give you that the statistical information that you are looking for. Setting it to zero means you are going to log every single statement sent to PostgreSQL. If you want to set it to be a little bit less aggressive than that, you can set the number above 0; the number is in milliseconds by default. You can see both the duration and the statement on the same log line like as follows:

```
LOG:  duration: 2008.448 ms  statement: select pg_sleep(2);
```

You will see the preceding log line in log files under the $PGDATA/pg_log (in PostgreSQL 9.6 or older) or $PGDATA/log (in PostgreSQL 10 or higher) directory.

This is really important for log analysis tools. If you're using log statement and log duration, you end up with those on two different lines, which becomes much more difficult to analyze.

Note   If you set this parameter to 0, it generates a log of log files if you have a busy database (where lots of queries are sent to the database). Make sure you have enough disk space for log files and have a retention to clean up unnecessary log files.

---

log_line_prefix

When reading logs, it's essential to know precisely when a query, action, or error occurred, which database it occurred in, which user called it, and which statements preceded it in the same transaction. For that reason, log_line_prefix should be properly configured so that this information is available.

The recommended value for this parameter is '%t [%p]: [%l-1] query=%u,user=%u,db=%d,app=%a,client=%h'.

%a	Application name
%u	User name
%d	Database name
%r	Remote host name or IP address, and remote port
%h	Remote host name or IP address
%p	Process ID
%t	Time stamp without milliseconds
%m	Time stamp with milliseconds
%i	Command tag: type of session's current command
%e	SQLSTATE error code
%c	Session ID
%l	Number of the log line for each session or process, starting at 1
%s	Process start time stamp
%v	Virtual transaction ID (backendID/localXID)
%x	Transaction ID (0 if none is assigned)
%q	Produces no output, but tells non-session processes to stop at this point in the string; ignored by session processes
%%	Literal %

It is essentially ripped from exactly what pgBadger is looking for by default, which I find to be a really good log line prefix. You can customize it if you want, and pg badger actually allows you two options to set it to whatever to configure it so that it knows what kind of log line prefix you have.

```
2019-12-03 10:13:41 IST [46369]: [7-1] query=postgres,user=p
ostgres,db=postgres,app=psql,client=[local] LOG:  duration:
2000.434 ms  statement: select pg_sleep(2);
```

In the preceding line, we have the timestamp (2019-12-03 10:13:41 IST); this is really important for being able to do an analysis across time of when a query ran. Process ID session and line number ([46369]: [7-1]) are pretty straightforward. The logged in user (user=postgres) is actually the user that logged into the database; if you change the user using something like set role, this doesn't update. It will still be the user that was logged in as. So, that is something to just be aware of when you're using that. The database that was logged into is db=postgres and app=psql is the application name if set. So, many people may not be aware that we have this capability to have the application name. If you are using the psql terminal, it will be set to "psql" or if it is pgAdmin, it will set it to "pgAdmin." But if you're writing your own custom code, you can have this set to essentially whatever you want for each database connection; that can be really handy for being able to break up your log file based on what applications are connecting. You can use the "application_name" parameter for that purpose.

log_checkpoints

A checkpoint is a database process that occurs in order to synchronize the database blocks in the buffer cache to data files on the disk. During a checkpoint, dirty pages from shared_buffers will be written to disk by the background writer, or as of PostgreSQL 9.2, the checkpointer process.

Checkpoints are very disrupting to your database performance and can cause connections to stall for up to a few seconds while they occur. Starting in PostgreSQL 8.3, you can get verbose logging of the checkpoint process by turning on log_checkpoints:

```
2019-12-03 10:16:32 IST [46135]: [6-1]
query=,user=,db=,app=,client= LOG:  checkpoint complete: wrote
64 buffers (0.4%); O WAL file(s) added, O removed, O recycled;
write=0.002 s, sync=0.002 s, total=0.008 s; sync files=16,
longest=0.000 s, average=0.000 s; distance=711 kB, estimate=711 kB
```

log_checkpoints is going to tell us all the information about when a checkpoint started, why it started, how long it ran, and a whole bunch of other really useful statistical information that tools like pgBadger can pick up and provide information to you about. You may go into a place where people are complaining that slow queries are happening—like every couple minutes or every few minutes. That is probably because every few minutes a checkpoint starts and we write out all of the data to disk. While we are writing out all of the data, the entire system ends up being slow or inquiries are slower, so that's something to be looking for. Sometimes you can correlate that between when the checkpoints are happening vs. when the queries are happening, which is really useful information

log_connections and log_disconnections

This is a straight-up connection logging information, just logging the connections and disconnections. It is pretty straightforward: really important and really useful but not too complicated.

Enabling these parameters, you end up with three log entries:

```
2019-12-03 10:17:47 IST [46595]: [1-1] query=[unknown],u
ser=[unknown],db=[unknown],app=[unknown],client=[local]
LOG:  connection received: host=[local]
```

```
2019-12-03 10:17:47 IST [46595]: [2-1] query=postgres,user=post
gres,db=postgres,app=[unknown],client=[local] LOG:  connection
authorized: user=postgres database=postgres
```

```
2019-12-03 10:18:33 IST [46595]: [3-1] query=postgres,user=pos
tgres,db=postgres,app=psql,client=[local] LOG:  disconnection:
session time: 0:00:45.725 user=postgres database=postgres
host=[local]
```

You get a connection received entry and then you get the actual authentication information when the connection's been authorized and then you get a disconnection. So, this can help you analyze how long connections have been made to the database; in particular, if you have a lot of short-lived connections, that's usually a bad thing. You actually want to use a connection pool. More about connection pool is covered in Chapter 7.

log_lock_waits

Logging of log_lock_waits is another really important one that people don't always realize. Your query slows because it may be waiting on a lock on a table or a row. This happens all the time and people don't know it. If you turn on log_lock_waits, after one second PostgreSQL does something called a deadlock check. It will run this deadlock checking routine, which looks to see if there are any deadlocks between the existing queries that are running. It will log lines like the following:

```
2019-12-03 10:21:46 IST [46729]: [4-1] query=postgres,user=pos
tgres,db=postgres,app=psql,client=[local] LOG:  process 46729
still waiting for ShareLock on transaction 573 after 1000.186 ms
```

```
2019-12-03 10:21:46 IST [46729]: [5-1] query=postgres,user=p
ostgres,db=postgres,app=psql,client=[local] DETAIL:  Process
holding the lock: 46705. Wait queue: 46729.
```

```
2019-12-03 10:21:46 IST [46729]: [6-1] query=postgres,user=p
ostgres,db=postgres,app=psql,client=[local] CONTEXT:  while
updating tuple (0,1) in relation "lock_test"
```

```
2019-12-03 10:21:46 IST [46729]: [7-1] query=postgres,user=po
stgres,db=postgres,app=psql,client=[local] STATEMENT:  update
lock_test set id=4;
```

The first line is saying that process 46729 is still waiting for this sharelock on transaction 573. After waiting around for a second deadlock timeout hit, we ran the deadlock checker and found out that we're waiting on a lock. We also know what's holding that lock. So, the process 46705 is holding the lock that we need. We also have the information about what kind of lock we are waiting on. This is very useful information for doing deadlock and lock analysis; if you don't have this enabled, it's definitely recommended to enable it.

log_temp_files

This parameter is to log the information about temp files. Whenever you have temp files being created, that means the database has to do some amount of disk IO.

```
2019-12-03 10:27:35 IST [46729]: [26-1] query=postgres,user=pos
tgres,db=postgres,app=psql,client=[local] LOG:  duration: 9.927
ms  statement: select * from temp_test order by id;
```

```
2019-12-03 10:27:40 IST [46729]: [27-1] query=postgres,
user=postgres,db=postgres,app=psql,client=[local] LOG:  temporary
file: path "base/pgsql_tmp/pgsql_tmp46729.1", size 147456
```

In the preceding case, you can see that the query ran is "select * from temp_test order by id;". So, what's happened is that we're doing a sort and it is using a temp file to do this sort. That tends to be expensive because it means you're going out to disk to do a sort. You can detect this and realize it by logging these temp files that PostgreSQL creates. You just set log temp files equal to 0 and then every time PostgreSQL creates a temp file when it's trying to run a query for anything, it's going to log information about what that query was. This can be really helpful for figuring out the reason behind slow queries that generate lot of temp files.

log_autovacuum_min_duration

Another thing that people often complain about is "autovacuum is running and it's vacuuming the stuff and it is killing my system and I want to stop it." Do not ever do that, for starters. It just becomes a real problem because you end up with a lot of bloat. We will cover more about bloat/vacuum in Chapter 6.

If you set log_autovacuum_min_duration to zero, then you can see a line like the following when autovacuum occurs on a table:

```
2019-12-03 10:30:28 IST [47078]: [1-1]
query=,user=,db=,app=,client= LOG:  automatic vacuum of table
"postgres.public.autovac_test": index scans: 0
        pages: 45 removed, 0 remain, 0 skipped due to pins, 0
        skipped frozen
        tuples: 10000 removed, 0 remain, 0 are dead but not yet
        removable, oldest xmin: 577
        buffer usage: 161 hits, 0 misses, 4 dirtied
        avg read rate: 0.000 MB/s, avg write rate: 6.793 MB/s
        system usage: CPU: user: 0.00 s, system: 0.00 s,
        elapsed: 0.00 s
```

You can see everything that VACUUM is doing across every table every time, and you get all of this wonderful information like how many dead tuples were found, how many it was able to mark as completely removed, and how many are dead but not removable.

Monitoring Databases

Logging is a key thing for monitoring. Lots of monitoring tools are dependent on logging information for monitoring. Monitoring helps you to identify issues proactively and resolve them before they actually happen.

More than how to monitor, we will learn what to monitor in this chapter. The intention is that there are lots of tools available on the market with detailed documentation on how to use them; however, it is important to know what to monitor first. So, we are going to discuss:

- Levels of monitoring

- OS level monitoring

- Database level monitoring

- Monitoring/reporting tools available

Levels of Monitoring

You cannot just monitor everything all the time, so there are various levels of monitoring:

- Every minute

- Every 5 mins

- Every hour

- Every 6 hours

- Daily once

- Weekly once

So, some values of some features you can monitor daily once, or weekly once is also fine. But some things like number of database sessions or load by each session you would ideally like to monitor every minute or 5 minutes. It will help your debugging in case of database issues. If you want to debug which session yesterday at 5 o'clock was taking more CPU and RAM and what it was running, then that particular historical data has to be present. Without the historical data, you cannot understand or cannot debug which sessions or what queries are impacted by the session and how many sessions are impacted. So, those parameters should be captured every minute or 5 minutes.

However, if you capture every minute, you will have more data in your monitoring system. This will impact the amount of data required in the monitoring system to capture and store it. So, usually depending on the storage space at your monitoring tool, decide whether it is 1 or 5 minutes and take it forward from there.

OS Level Monitoring

You should have OS level monitoring, as sometimes the reason behind the slowness of a database is OS hardware or resource utilization. So, what should be monitored at the OS level? And how should it be monitored?

- CPU

- Memory (RAM/SWAP)

- IO

- Network

- Filesystem

You can monitor all hardware-related metrics through the "sar" command as explained in the "sar" subsection of the "Monitoring/Reporting Tools" section later in the chapter.

CPU

While monitoring CPU utilization, you should look at idle time, user CPU usage, how much the system is using, total CPU usage, and how many CPU context switches. If there are more context switches, it is likely you don't have enough cores to handle your processes.

Memory

Keep an eye on RAM and swap usage. If swap is getting used, monitor how many swap-ins or swap-outs are happening and page-ins or page-outs are happening. This helps in knowing whether memory is sufficient or you need to add additional memory.

IO

You should monitor your input/output operations per second (IOPS). It tells you how much read/write is happening with your hard disk, which helps to know if your app is more read/write intensive. If there are more reads, your system is slow because the amount of data requested is high. You have to monitor IO to know this information.

You would then know the system you have is enough to support required IOPS or needs upgrade.

Network

Monitor the network to see how much data is going in and out. If the user is requesting huge data flowing in and out of the system, your network may get stuck. You need to monitor how much network input and output is happening so that you can allocate network bandwidth accordingly.

Filesystem

Monitor filesystem space usage so that you can avoid database down issues when it is full. This is proactive monitoring. You can set an alarm on 70% or 80% full and when the alarm raises, you can add more storage or remove unnecessary things from the filesystem.

Database Level Monitoring

So, we are going to talk about what should be monitored at the database level. Let us differentiate on the basis of frequency of monitoring.

Frequent Monitoring

The following database information needs frequent monitoring every minute or 5 minutes:

- Active session
- Inactive session
- Long-running query (session query running time)
- Locks
- Waiting sessions
- SQL queries being run
- CPU and memory occupied by each session
- Number of connections
- Primary/standby delay
- Any errors in logs

Daily or Weekly Basis

Other database-related information that can be monitored on a daily or weekly basis is:

- Database size

- Tablespace size

- Object (table/index) size

- Last vacuum/autovacuum

- Last analyze/auto analyzed

- Bloat on table/indexes

- Number of checkpoints

- Number of wal files generated

It is very important to monitor how frequently your db/tablespace/ objects are growing. It helps in capacity planning, like how much data will increase in the next few years. If you have this data, you can plan for it. If you are monitoring through a tool, then select a tool that has the feature of monitoring it.

Monitor how frequently VACUUM is running and when was the last vacuum/analyze run. Based on this, you can make sure current autovacuum settings are enough or you can reconfigure autovacuum or analyze settings. It helps in performance improvement.

Monitoring bloat helps to remove the bloat on table/index and improve performance. Another advantage is you can remove space if you see object size is huge due to bloat.

Frequent checkpoints impact performance. If checkpoints are happening at a high rate, the issue would be loading too much data or lots of update/delete. So, this information helps to investigate the issues.

If data load is huge, it generates a lot of wals, which is a lot of IO and space. So, you can tune parameters to reduce the generation.

Monitoring/Reporting Tools

There are various methods of monitoring a production system that can be used to identify issues with system load and throughput. There are many open source or enterprise tools available on the market for monitoring. Tools information is available here: `https://wiki.postgresql.org/wiki/Monitoring`.

Here are some tools you can consider using. We are not going to cover all the tools, but a few:

- pgBadger

- pgCluu

- sar

- pg_buffercache

- Nagios

- Zabbix

- datadog

pgBadger

pgBadger is a log-analysis tool specifically for PostgreSQL. It produces a detailed report of activity on the database server (or at least activity that makes it into the log files), including temp files, slow queries, VACUUM operations, connections, and many other sets of information. It's always advised to use the latest version, as it will contain fixes and the latest analysis features.

It can be downloaded from here: `https://pgbadger.darold.net/`.

It's often necessary to enable various logging parameters ahead of time for the reports to contain useful information. These are typically:

```
logging_collector = on
log_line_prefix = '%t [%p]: [%l-1] user=%u,db=%d '
log_min_duration_statement = 2s
log_checkpoints = on
log_connections = on
log_disconnections = on
log_lock_waits = on
log_temp_files = 0
log_autovacuum_min_duration = 0
```

Don't use the preceding values blindly, but adjust each setting to be appropriate to the customer's system. Setting certain parameters too low (like log_min_duration_statement) could adversely affect database performance on a live system due to a very high volume of logging.

pgCluu

pgCluu monitors an entire cluster for performance metrics, such as the utilization of CPU, memory, swap, system load, number of processes, block IO, changes in the size of individual databases, database connections, temporary files, and many other measurements. It can be downloaded from here: https://github.com/darold/pgcluu.

It comes in two parts: the collector process (pgcluu_collectd) and the report-generating tool (pgcluu).

Typical usage would be:

```
mkdir /tmp/stat_db/
pgcluu_collectd -D -i 60 /tmp/stat_db/ -h localhost -d postgres
```

This would start collecting data every 60 seconds. Collection would stop with:

```
pgcluu_collectd -k
```

You'd then generate the report:

```
mkdir /tmp/report_db/
pgcluu -o /tmp/report_db/ /tmp/stat_db/
```

That directory will then contain an HTML report that can be opened in the browser. All files in that directory will be needed.

sar

sar (meaning System Activity Report) monitors CPU activity, memory, paging, device load, and network activity. It's readily available (and usually already running) on most modern Linux installations via the sysstat package; this makes it very useful for situations where the customer either doesn't have monitoring set up or won't let you access it.

Find out if sar is already enabled and running by checking for collected data in /var/log/sa (CentOS) or /var/log/sysstat (Ubuntu). saXX files are binary data; sarXX are converted text.

Check the poll cycle by looking at the appropriate crontab in /etc/cron.d/sysstat. The default is 10 minutes; determine if this is frequent enough for your purposes.

Verify that collection of disk stats is enabled in the config file: /etc/sysconfig/sysstat (CentOS) or /etc/default/sysstat (Ubuntu). You should find an OPTIONS parameter set to "-S DISK."

If sar is already running, you can just use the already collected statistics. Only the binary data files will hold the most recent poll; the conversion to text only happens once daily, so if you want immediate stats, you need to run the conversion yourself.

If sar is not running, you can manually collect the data:

```
sar [stats options] -o [output_file] [poll interval in seconds]
[number of polls]
```

127

An example is:

```
sar -A -o my_cool_stats 60 30
```

   -A = collect all stats

   -o = store stats in this file (in binary format)

   60 = collect every 60 seconds

   30 = collect 30 times

Note that the -A option generates about 18MB of data per poll; plan space accordingly.

You can then use the following command to generate a report:

```
sar -A -f my_cool_stats > my_cool_stats.txt
```

Note that the conversion from binary to text must be run on a machine with the same architecture as the collector. Usually you will do the conversion on the same machine that did the collection.

Here are useful options, if you don't want to collect all stats with -A.

-b	for IO stats – can be useful in tuning checkpoint_completion_target and checkpoint_segments.
-dp	activity per block device; pretty-print the block names (must use -S DISK or -A when collecting) you REALLY REALLY want to pretty-print them
-n	"DEV,EDEV" network stats, including errors
-r	memory
-S	swap
-u	CPU usage (or -P "ALL" for CPU usage per process) – high % of system time may indicate an issue with Transparent Huge Page compaction
-w	context switching
-W	pages swapped – a spike here may indicate tuning of shared_buffers and work_mem/max_connections may be needed

What this looks like:

```
sar -bdprSuwW -n "DEV,EDEV" -f my_cool_stats > my_cool_stats.txt
```

The text data can be further analyzed in a spreadsheet or other graphing tools.

You can also generate a graphical report directly from the binary data using isag, ksar tools.

More information about data collection and conversion can be found in the sar man pages.

pg_buffercache

The pg_buffercache extension is useful to monitor which relations are occupying space in shared memory. Permission will need to be obtained from the customer before installing any extension such as this, and in many cases it may not be possible to do so. If you do install it, it only needs to be installed in one database, which can be one that isn't used for any production data.

Storing the results of the query that uses the pg_buffercache view provided by this extension into a text file can reveal buffer page eviction issues. This is where a single query might push out all pages frequently used in the cache, meaning they need to be loaded back in, resulting in periods where queries run slower. If you do this, ensure you output the timestamp to see if there's any correlation between those results and the ones from pgBadger.

This is an example, where the query used to gather the buffer cache data is put into a file at /tmp/pg_buffercache.sql. The query we'll be using is as follows:

```
SELECT now(), d.datname, c.relname, count(*) AS buffers
FROM pg_buffercache b INNER JOIN pg_class c
        ON b.relfilenode = pg_relation_filenode(c.oid)
INNER JOIN pg_database d
        ON b.reldatabase = d.oid
GROUP BY d.datname, c.relname
ORDER BY 4 DESC
LIMIT 10;
```

We then call the file using psql, request comma-separated output, and append the results to a file. On Unix/Linux systems systems, we could then run:

```
while [ true ]; do psql -AtX -F ',' -f /tmp/pg_buffercache.sql
postgres >> /tmp/pg_buffercache.log;sleep 5;done
```

This would produce an output for buffers every 5 seconds.

Summary

In this chapter, we covered why logging is important and how to log and what information to log. We have also talked about what to consider while turning on the logging parameters and how to use the information logged. We have covered monitoring procedures, including what to monitor and how frequent monitoring is required. In the next chapter, we will talk about what is bloat in the database and how it can be removed. And we will cover what are the best practices to execute maintenance activities like VACUUM and reindex in detail.

CHAPTER 6

Execute Maintenance

In the last chapter, we talked about the importance of logging and how to/when to/what to log. We looked at different logging parameters and their use cases. And we covered what should be monitored at the OS and database level, and details about a few monitoring tools. In this chapter, we will start with the MVCC concept in PostgreSQL and will continue with the maintenance activities in PostgreSQL and how to schedule them based on information available. We will also look at how autovacuum and VACUUM works in PostgreSQL and how to improve the performance of the database. We will also cover another important maintenance activity which is REINDEX.

What is MVCC

Multiversion concurrency control (MVCC) is currently the most popular transaction management scheme in modern database management systems (DBMSs). Although MVCC was designed in the late 1970s, it is used in almost every major relational DBMS released in the last decade. Maintaining multiple versions of data potentially increases parallelism without sacrificing serializability when processing transactions.

MVCC in PostgreSQL

To understand how MVCC perform when processing transactions in modern hardware settings, we need to understand four key design decisions: concurrency control protocol, version storage, garbage

© Baji Shaik 2020
B. Shaik, *PostgreSQL Configuration*, https://doi.org/10.1007/978-1-4842-5663-3_6

collection, and index management. Concurrency control protocol talks about how concurrent sessions in a database can be managed. This is where you see different transaction levels. Version storage is storing different versions of data. PostgreSQL stores old and new versions of data in case of update/delete. Garbage collection is a process to remove old versions of data. Index management is a way to store the index data.

Here is an example to understand MVCC in practical terms. Every statement that modifies the database generates a transaction ID, which is represented by a pseudo column xid within each table. And there are a couple of other pseudo columns, xmin and xmax, which represent transaction IDs depending on the status of the row.

Consider a table "test" with one column. Now see what happens if a row is inserted:

```
postgres=# CREATE TABLE test(ID int);
CREATE TABLE
postgres=# INSERT INTO test VALUES(1);
INSERT 0 1
postgres=# SELECT  xmin, xmax, id FROM test;
 xmin | xmax | id
------+------+----
 1739 |    0 |  1
(1 row)
```

So, xmin represents the xid (transaction ID) through which the row was inserted and xmax is always 0 for visible rows. xmax > 0 represents an expired row, which is not visible.

There are some cases where xmax > 0, but still the row is visible. It is possible if you update/delete something in a transaction and it is rolled back.

If the Row Is Deleted

The row gets deleted and a version of that row still appears to maintain the MVCC. In this scenario, for the deleted row, xmin is the xid of the INSERT statement through which the row was inserted and xmax becomes the xid of DELETE statement through which the row was deleted.

If the Row Is Updated

In PostgreSQL, UPDATE is considered as DELETE + INSERT. The old row gets deleted and the new row gets inserted. Both the rows are maintained to fulfil MVCC. In this scenario, for the old row, xmin is the xid through which the row was inserted and xmax is the xid through which the row was updated. For the new row, xmin is the xid through which the row was updated and xmax is 0, as the row is visible.

Figure 6-1 illustrates MVCC behavior.

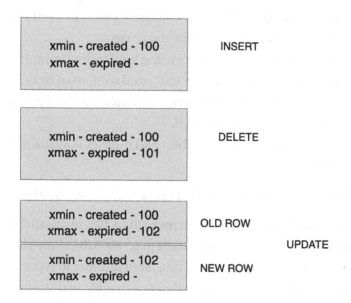

Figure 6-1. *MVCC behavior*

Why/How—Maintenance Activities

The first question that comes to mind when we hear about maintenance is "why would we need maintenance at all?" As explained in the "MVCC in PostgreSQL" section, PostgreSQL uses different row versions as a part of MVCC behavior. So, when you DELETE or UPDATE a table, it creates two versions of data, in which one is visible and the other is invisible. Those invisible rows, which we call "dead tuples" (we call it table/index bloat as well), need to be cleaned up. This is where we need maintenance.

The next part of the question is "how can we do maintenance?" VACUUM is a process to clean up dead tuples.

Table and Index Bloat

Table and index bloat is caused by deleted or updated rows not being VACUUMed. This means that such rows will occupy space and cannot be reused until cleaned up. Such a state can cause tables to swell in size, even if only UPDATEs are issued against the database.

The causes of this are either locks being held by long-running transactions (although this has been mitigated somewhat since PostgreSQL 8.4), or the autovacuum configuration for the database and/or specific tables isn't aggressive enough.

A query to get the most bloats tables and indexes is available in PostgreSQL wiki:

`https://wiki.postgresql.org/wiki/Show_database_bloat`.

If there are tables or indexes with more than 10% bloat, and where the number of wasted bytes is significant (e.g., 200MB), these should be included in the report. Should there be a large number to report, put them into a separate text file instead and reference that file in the report, which should then be provided to the customer along with the final report.

AUTOVACUUM/VACUUM

Let us talk about AUTOVACUUM a bit.

- What does autovacuum do?

- How does autovacuum work?

- What else important can autovacuum daemon do

- autovacuum parameters

- VACUUM strategies

- autovacuum IO overhead

What Does Autovacuum Do?

Modern (classical) databases must deal with two fundamental problems:

- *Concurrent operations*: For that they can use transactions.

- *Failures*: For that they can recover to the last successful transaction using WAL.

To live with the first problem, concurrent operations, databases usually implement some kind of concurrency scheduling algorithms and transactions. The second problem is failures; if something goes wrong, we usually have a WAL algorithm for PostgreSQL.

Technically, that means there is a combination of locking and MVCC algorithms that provides transactions support. Undo and redo information is stored somewhere to make recovery possible. PostgreSQL keeps redo like many other databases in WAL, but undo is kept a bit nontraditional. It is kept in data files itself. For example, Oracle has some undo information and special segments that are called undo segments, and db2 stores some undo information in modern Linux versions.

Due to this kind of undo mechanism, PostgreSQL needs to deal with the garbage collection process called VACUUM. Tuples that are not visible to any running transaction should be removed. Otherwise, fragmentation increases and you run into bloat.

VACUUM removes all pages that are not visible to any running transaction. You need to run VACUUM very frequently to prevent bloat. If you don't, you will need VACUUM FULL. It rebuilds the table, which can be painful. Autovacuum automates VACUUM process.

How Does Autovacuum Work?

There are two different kinds of autovacuum systems: the autovacuum launcher and the auotvacuum worker.

Let us look at how the flow works:

- The auotvacuum launcher is a continuous running process, which is started by the postmaster.

- The launcher schedules autovacuum workers to start when needed.

- The auotvacuum worker process is the actual process that does the vacuuming. They connect to a database that is determined by the launcher and, once connected, they read the catalog tables to select a table as a candidate for vacuuming.

- There is an autovacuum shared memory area, where the launcher stores information about the tables in a database that needs a VACUUM.

- When the autovacuum launcher wants a new worker to start, it sets a flag in the shared memory and sends a signal to the postmaster.

- Then the postmaster starts a worker. This new worker process connects to the shared memory and reads the information in the autovacuum shared memory area stored by the launcher process and does its work.

What Else of Importance Can the Autovacuum Daemon Do?

Besides vacuuming, autovacuum also:

- Collects statistics for the optimizer (autoanalyze)

- Performs transaction wraparound autovacuum

Autovacuum Parameters

Basically, two things that might make DBAs not so happy are seeing a database with auto VACUUM switched off or autovacuum with default settings. There are a lot of ideas about how to improve the performance of the database, but turning off the autovacuum is definitely not one of them. It is not always recommended to leave autovacuum settings at default values.

If your autovacuum process runs for hours and interferes with some data definition language (DDL) statements like ALTER/TRUNCATE, to simply terminate it is not an option. It will just postpone the VACUUM, and work will be cumulated. Especially for online transaction processing (OLTP), autovacuum should be configured aggressively enough so it can work with small portions of data quickly.

If you see the settings of autovacuum, they look something like this:

```
postgres=# select name, setting, context  from pg_settings
where category ~ 'Autovacuum';
                    name                  | setting   | context
------------------------------------------+-----------+------------
 autovacuum                               | on        | sighup
 autovacuum_analyze_scale_factor          | 0.1       | sighup
 autovacuum_analyze_threshold             | 50        | sighup
 autovacuum_freeze_max_age                | 200000000 | postmaster
 autovacuum_max_workers                   | 3         | postmaster
 autovacuum_multixact_freeze_max_age      | 400000000 | postmaster
 autovacuum_naptime                       | 60        | sighup
 autovacuum_vacuum_cost_delay             | 20        | sighup
 autovacuum_vacuum_cost_limit             | -1        | sighup
 autovacuum_vacuum_scale_factor           | 0.2       | sighup
 autovacuum_vacuum_threshold              | 50        | sighup
(11 rows)
```

autovacuum

This should nearly always be set to on, otherwise no autovacuuming will occur in the database, and there will certainly need to be routine manual vacuums applied.

autovacuum_max_workers

The default of 3 tends to be too low for anything except small database systems. This should probably be set to something within the 6 to 12 range, leaning more to the latter if there are a lot of tables with frequent updates or deletes.

autovacuum_naptime

It is minimum delay between autovacuum runs. The default of 1 min may be sufficient for some systems, but on busier ones with many writes, it may be beneficial to increase this to stop autovacuum waking up too often.

This should also be increased on systems with many databases, as this setting determines the wake-up time per database. An autovacuum worker process will begin as frequently as autovacuum_naptime / number of databases.

For example, if autovacuum_naptime = 1 min (60 seconds), and there were 60 databases, an autovacuum worker process would be started every second (60 seconds / 60 databases = 1 second). However, tuning this setting too high can result in more work needed to be done in each vacuuming round.

autovacuum_vacuum_threshold / autovacuum_analyze_threshold

These both determine the minimum number of rows in a table that need to have changed in order for the table to be scheduled for an autovacuum and an autoanalyze, respectively. The default for both is 50, which is very low for most tables.

autovacuum_vacuum_scale_factor / autovacuum_analyze_scale_factor

These both determine the percentage of a table that needs to have changes in order for the table to be scheduled for an autovacuum and an autoanalyze, respectively. The default for the autovacuum_vacuum_scale_factor is 0.2 (meaning 20%), and the autovacuum_analyze_scale_factor is 0.1 (meaning 10%). Both of these figures are fine for tables of a modest size (up to around 500MB), but for larger tables they are too high. If, for example, there was a table that was 120GB in size, 24GB (20% of 120GB) worth of dead tuples would have to exist before they can start being cleaned up, which would be a lot of vacuuming work once it kicks in. However, if large tables are in the minority on the database, it's better to set these parameters on the table level rather than in the config file.

autovacuum_vacuum_cost_delay

This defaults to 20ms, which is very conservative and can prevent VACUUM from keeping up with changes. This should nearly always be decreased, in many cases to as low as 2 ms. It may need to be tested with various settings to see what's needed to keep up.

VACUUM Strategies

It is important to ensure that tables are being regularly VACUUMed. The most useful starting metric is to ensure that all tables have been VACUUMed at least once every 7 days (one week).

Although this number may need to be adjusted up or down, it is the best starting point.

```
SELECT schemaname,
       relname,
       now() - last_autovacuum AS "noautovac",
       now() - last_vacuum AS "novac",
       n_tup_upd,
       n_tup_del,
       pg_size_pretty(pg_total_relation_size(schemaname||'.'
       ||relname)),
       autovacuum_count,
       last_autovacuum,
       vacuum_count,
       last_vacuum
  FROM pg_stat_user_tables
 WHERE (now() - last_autovacuum > '7 days'::interval
```

```
        OR now() - last_vacuum >'7 days'::interval )
        OR (last_autovacuum IS NULL AND last_vacuum IS NULL )
 ORDER BY  novac DESC;
```

This list will provide a view to all of the tables and their VACUUM need. If the list returns with a no rows, it means that all tables have been VACUUMed within the last 7 days. The targetlist generated (if any) should be prioritized by number of updates and deletes.

Manual VACUUM

One way of dealing with this table list is to manually run the command "VACUUM VERBOSE <table>" against each of those tables. This will run an unthrottled VACUUM of the table and provide output stats.

Throttle VACUUM

Although VACUUM doesn't perform any blocking / locking operations, it does perform a deep-scan of a table; this can cause an added stress to the IO (and caching) subsystems. If the impact of VACUUM begins to affect performance, you can cancel a running VACUUM by either ctrl+c or:

```
SELECT pid,
        state,
         query
 FROM pg_stat_activity
 WHERE query like '%VACUU%'
   AND state = 'active';
```

Take the PID that you find, and run:

```
select pg_terminate_backend(pid);
```

From here, you can throttle VACUUM by setting the "vacuum_cost_delay" parameter in just your session:

```
postgres=# set vacuum_cost_delay=10;
SET
postgres=# VACUUM VERBOSE pgbench_branches ;
INFO: vacuuming "public.pgbench_branches"
INFO: index "pgbench_branches_pkey" now contains 10 row
versions in 2 pages DETAIL: 0 index row versions were removed.
0 index pages have been deleted, 0 are currently reusable.
CPU 0.00s/0.00u sec elapsed 0.00 sec.
INFO: "pgbench_branches": found 0 removable, 10 nonremovable
row versions in 1 out of DETAIL: 0 dead row versions cannot be
removed yet.
There were 0 unused item pointers.
0 pages are entirely empty.
CPU 0.00s/0.00u sec elapsed 0.00 sec.
VACUUM
postgres=#
```

You can increment the cost delay in increments of 10 to increase the amount of throttle you would like to enforce. It is possible (but not recommended) to change this setting globally. Setting this like the preceding will only affect your session and will reset when you close the connection.

Schedule

To schedule this job, psql could be used to execute a job. Create an SQL file (for example - vacuum.sql)

```
--set vacuum_cost_delay=
 VACUUM VERBOSE ANALYZE table1;
 VACUUM VERBOSE ANALYZE table2;
 VACUUM VERBOSE ANALYZE table3;
 etc...
```

Then, it can be run using psql from any host:

```
psql -h <server_ip> -f vacuum.sql -U <user> -d <db> >>
/log/vacuum.log
```

This could be done more dynamically. Create an sql file using the following command (for example, gen_vacuum_list.sql):

```
SELECT 'VACUUM VERBOSE ANALYZE ' || schemaname || '.' ||
relname ||';'
FROM pg_stat_user_tables
WHERE (now() - last_autovacuum > '7 days'::interval
        OR now() - last_vacuum >'7 days'::interval )
        OR (last_autovacuum IS NULL AND last_vacuum IS NULL );
```

Dump the output to a file, and execute the result against the database:

```
psql -h <server_ip> -f gen_vacuum_list.sql -U <user> -d
<db>  >> /tmp/vacuum_tables.sql
```

```
psql -h <server_ip> -f /tmp/vacuum_tables.sql -U <user> -d
<db>  >> /log/vacuum.log
```

autovacuum IO

Autovacuum has its own mechanism to reduce IO overhead.

Autovacuum delays autovacuum_naptime seconds, then checks if tables need a VACUUM. It runs VACUUM on a table until autovacuum_vacuum_cost_limit is reached, then sleeps: autovacuum_vacuum_cost_delay milliseconds.

This might not be a good algorithm, mostly because it was designed for all the hardware. For example, it does not differentiate the logical and physical IO. So, it may be IO from disk or IO from shared memory; autovacuum behavior is the same for these mechanisms. So, the results can be confusing. Modern SSDs are quite fast. So, such kinds of external regulation of IO are not so necessary for them.

If you have slow disks, you can actually trick a bit by increasing the amount of autovacuum_workers. Because autovacuum has three workers by default, they begin to work with several tables. When they are vacuuming these tables, actually the autovacuum_vacuum_scale_factor comes in and probably the next table should be vacuumed for 1% of its data changed. But due to a shortage of autovacuum workers, it cannot be vacuumed at that point. By the time autovacuum workers are available, this table data might change to 50% or 80%. This will increase the work for autovacuum, which then, gets slow down. It actually depends on how many CPUs you have for autovacuum workers though.

Another idea is to keep autovacuum_vacuum_cost_delay lower, maybe at 10. Lower than 10 effectively does not help a lot but your autovacuum workers will work as intensively as they can. PostgreSQL will not regulate its IO activity in any way; in that case, you can try to regulate the activity externally using ionice and renice on autovacuum workers on a regular basis.

In crontab:

```
* * * * * /usr/bin/pgrep -f 'postgres: autovacuum' | xargs
--no-run-if-empty -I $ renice -n 20 -p $ >/dev/null 2>/dev/null
* * * * * /usr/bin/pgrep -f 'postgres: autovacuum' | xargs
--no-run-if-empty -I $ ionice -c 3 -t -p $
```

In postgresql.conf:

```
autovacuum_max_workers = 20
autovacuum_vacuum_cost_delay = 10
```

Keep in mind that ionice could not work if you have a non-CFQ (Completely Fair Queuing) scheduler on Linux.

Index Fragmentation

Indexes can become fragmented over time the more they are updated. This affects performance, and such indexes should be REINDEXed in order to optimize their use. One way to identify index fragmentation is to use the pgstattuple extension. If the customer grants you permission to install it, you can use the pgstatindex function it provides like so:

```
postgres=# create table index_test (id int);
CREATE TABLE
postgres=# insert into index_test values (generate_series(1,10000000));
INSERT 0 10000000
postgres=# create index fragmented_index on index_test (id);
CREATE INDEX
postgres=#
postgres=# create extension pgstattuple ;
CREATE EXTENSION
postgres=# insert into index_test values (generate_series(1,10000000));
INSERT 0 10000000
postgres=# update index_test set id = 1 where id < 5000000;
UPDATE 4999999
postgres=# SELECT * FROM pgstatindex('fragmented_index');
-[ RECORD 1 ]------+----------
version            | 2
tree_level         | 2
index_size         | 366919680
root_block_no      | 412
internal_pages     | 177
leaf_pages         | 44612
empty_pages        | 0
deleted_pages      | 0
avg_leaf_density   | 82.79
leaf_fragmentation | 35.65
```

This shows that the index named "frangmented_index" is 35.65% fragmented (as shown for leaf_fragmentation). On small indexes, this may not be such an issue, but on larger indexes it can noticeably degrade performance and occupy unnecessary space. A REINDEX would defragment the index and therefore also reduce its size:

```
postgres=# reindex index fragmented_index ;
REINDEX
Time: 7960.823 ms (00:07.961)
postgres=# SELECT * FROM pgstatindex('fragmented_index');
-[ RECORD 1 ]------+----------
version            | 2
tree_level         | 2
index_size         | 224641024
root_block_no      | 290
internal_pages     | 98
leaf_pages         | 27323
empty_pages        | 0
deleted_pages      | 0
avg_leaf_density   | 90.09
leaf_fragmentation | 0
```

As you can see, in this example the leaf_fragmentation shows that there's now no fragmentation in the index, and index_size has gone from 366919680 bytes to 224641024bytes, reducing its size by almost half.

If using PostgreSQL 9.3 or above, you can use the following query to get the details for every index at once:

```
SELECT a.indexrelname, b.*
FROM pg_stat_user_indexes a,
LATERAL pgstatindex(indexrelname) b
ORDER BY leaf_fragmentation DESC;
```

For previous versions, use:

```
SELECT (x.a).indexrelname, (x.b).*
FROM (SELECT a, pgstatindex(a.indexrelname) AS b
     FROM pg_stat_user_indexes a) x
ORDER BY leaf_fragmentation DESC;
```

However, on production system it is difficult to perform costly operations like REINDEX, as this acquires various locks on the objects. It is not advisable to rebuild indexes during peak times, and planning is required for such operations. Plan such costly operations whenever there will be a downtime for the application and database at the organizational level. REINDEX acquires various locks on the objects and performs dropping and recreating the index. PostgreSQL 8.2 onwards indexes can be created concurrently as well if required.

REINDEX rebuilds an index using the data stored in the index's table, replacing the old copy of the index.

There are two main reasons to use REINDEX:

- An index has become corrupted, and no longer contains valid data. REINDEX provides a recovery method.

- The index contains a lot of mostly empty index pages that are not being reclaimed. REINDEX provides a way to reduce the space consumption of the index by writing a new version of the index without the dead pages.

Note If you suspect corruption of an index on a user table, you can simply rebuild that index, or all indexes on the table, using REINDEX INDEX or REINDEX TABLE.

It is also recommended to perform ANALYZE after DDL changes or REINDEX operations. PostgreSQL 9.0 provides a command-line tool "reindexdb" that performs the same function. For more information on reindexing, see: `www.postgresql.org/docs/current/static/sql-reindex.html`.

Other Database Maintenance

As a part of maintenance, it is recommended to get rid of:

- Unused indexes
- Duplicate indexes

Unused Indexes

Indexes that aren't used add maintenance overhead to the tables they belong to and occupy space. As such, we should recommend that such indexes are dropped.

A query to identify these indexes is as follows:

```
SELECT relname AS table, indexrelname AS index, pg_size_
pretty(pg_relation_size(indexrelid)) AS size
FROM pg_stat_user_indexes
WHERE idx_scan = 0
ORDER BY pg_relation_size(indexrelid) DESC;
```

If there are a large number of results (e.g., more than 15 rows), they should be provided in a text file separate from the report. The results are ordered by size so that the indexes occupying the most space are listed first.

The benefits to removing redundant indexes are that they will free up space, and will improve the performance of updates, deletions, and insertions into tables because the indexes will no longer need to be updated with those changes.

The decision to remove a particular index might be mitigated by several possible factors:

- The traffic pattern currently in use does not cause the indexes to be used, but anticipated changes would cause them to be used.

- The planner is not properly using all the indexes it is expected to. There are unusual cases where the query execution planner should be using an index for execution of SQL DML, but does not. In these cases the index should not be removed, and the SQL in question examined and possibly restructured to properly use the index.

Duplicate Indexes

Duplicate indexes result in wasting space and increase overhead on table updates. The following query will return duplicate indexes, but the indexes may still differ in subtle ways, such as they could use a different collation or index access method (btree, hash, gin, gist), so they should be manually compared:

```
SELECT indrelid::regclass AS table, indkey AS column_numbers,
array_agg(indexrelid::regclass) AS indexes, pg_catalog.pg_get_
expr(indpred, indrelid, true) AS expression
FROM pg_index
GROUP BY indrelid, indkey, pg_catalog.pg_get_expr(indpred,
indrelid, true)
HAVING count(*) > 1;
```

This will return a row for each set of apparent duplicates, and an array of duplicate indexes will be displayed in the "indexes" column.

Summary

In this chapter, we have talked about MVCC in PostgreSQL, and how it causes bloat in the database and how it can be removed. We explained autovacuum work and its uses in detail. And we have covered the best practices to execute maintenance activities like VACUUM and reindex in detail. In the next chapter, we will talk about the importance of High Availability and procedures to implement it in PostgreSQL. We will cover some open source and enterprise tools to implement High Availability. We will also cover the importance of a pooler, and available poolers in the market and their implementation.

High Availability Procedures and Implementing a Pooler

In the last chapter, we talked about some basic things about MVCC in PostgreSQL, and what is bloat in the database and how it can be removed. We explained how autovacuum helps in removing bloat and improving performance. We also covered the best practices to execute maintenance activities like VACUUM and reindex in detail. In this chapter, we will talk about the importance of High Availability (HA), and what information we need to build an HA solution and the procedures to implement it in PostgreSQL. We will cover some open source and enterprise tools to implement HA. We will also cover the importance of a pooler, and available poolers on the market and their implementation.

© Baji Shaik 2020
B. Shaik, *PostgreSQL Configuration*, https://doi.org/10.1007/978-1-4842-5663-3_7

Why High Availability?

This is a basic question that every DBA should answer. HA is to protect your database from failures and helps in disaster recoveries. What exactly does the "protection" mean? It is not a kind of repairing of the failed data, but rather making data available for business in any way or at any cost. If your database is unavailable due to some reason, you will have to make sure that you have something to continue your application running with the same data. Reasons for database failures could be:

- Due to a disaster

- Database crash and not starting up

- Database is unavailable due to heavy load

- Database is corrupted due to bad disk or bad hardware

Gather Information to Set Up HA

Before setting up HA, we need to know what information is required. If you have the right information, based on that you can suggest a HA solution. So, here are few questions that you can ask your customer, to build the solution. Every question has a purpose that helps in architecting:

Q1.   What are your expectations for this HA solution?

Purpose: This is a basic question that you need answers to. You should ask about customer expectations on HA solutions of PostgreSQL. Customers come from different database backgrounds and they expect similar kinds of solutions are possible in PostgreSQL. It might not be possible sometimes. PostgreSQL has its own HA implementations and may not match with other databases' procedures all the time. So, if customers have the same kind of expectations as their previous databases (in case they are migrating from some enterprise databases), then you should explain possibilities and set expectations.

Q2. What are your primary server specs?

Purpose: It is very important to know about the customer's primary server specs so that you can suggest a similar kind of hardware for standby servers as well. The reason behind having similar hardware is if you do a failover, you would expect the same behavior and performance on a newly promoted standby server as well. So, if you have the same hardware on both primary and standby, you don't see much difference in performance after the failover.

Q3. How many standby servers do you want?

Purpose: The number of standby servers depends on customer choice. If they have a critical database and need HA across their data centers as well, then you would need to design a solution according to that. We will be discussing a solution related to it in this chapter.

Q4. How critical is your data?

Purpose: Like the previous question, if they have a critical database, you should suggest more standby servers than one and more data centers than one. Of course, you will have to take care of latencies for different data centers.

Q5. What are your RPO and RTO?

Purpose: This is very critical part at business level.
We should know the RTO and RPO in detail first
and then ask the customer for their expectations.
Based on the values, you can design your solution or
convince the customer if it is something that can't
be achieved. RTO (recovery time objective) and RPO
(recovery point objective) are explained in the next
section.

Q6. Is it a single data center or more than one?

Purpose: The customer may not be able to share
the details of their data centers until we specifically
ask them. So, this question helps us to know about
their data centers and implement cross-center
replications if needed.

Q7. If you have more than one data center, how far apart
are they?

Purpose: If the customer wants a solution across
different data centers, you would need to know how
far apart they are located so that you would analyze
the replication lag upfront. You can explain to the
customer about lags between data centers,

Q8. Are you specifically looking for any replication
solution?

Purpose: The customer has already done some
research and come up with some solutions
that include open source or enterprise tools for
implementation. You will need to look at the
architecture and the tools and let the customer

know if there are any known issues or limitations using their architecture and tools. If needed, you may want to redesign the solution.

Q9.   Do you open standby servers for read connections?

Purpose: PostgreSQL supports standby servers for read purposes. So, if the customer is unaware it, you may want to suggest read queries to standby servers to reduce the load on the primary. However, if the primary data is encrypted over the connections while reading, you should let the customer know and use the same process to pull the data.

Q10.   Do you want auto-failover solutions?

Purpose: Auto failover is something that PostgreSQL doesn't have in-built. You may want to create a few scripts to do that, or there are a lot of tools available on the market that you can use as a part of your solution. We will be talking about the tools in the next sections of this chapter.

Q11.   How much is the maximum delay that you are expecting between the primary and standby?

Purpose: Some customers use standby servers for read purposes. The way they use them could be to modify data in the primary and retrieve it immediately from the standby. If there is any lag between the primary and standby, you will see different data than expected. So, if you get the details of how they are querying, you can suggest timings to query if there is any lag that is expected.

RPO and RTO

These are typical business items that need to be taken care of when you are setting up HA solutions.

RPO (Recovery Point Objective)

This represents the point to which you can stand to lose data at any moment. It involves size of the data, that is, at the time of recovery in disaster situations, how much data loss you can afford.

Sometimes, the standby may be behind (lag) the primary. In that case, if you need a failover, it may lose some data that is not replicated to the standby. So, test your solution with a production load and analyze how much lag you see at any point. That will become your RPO.

RTO (Recovery Time Objective)

It is all about 9s. It represents how long the application can be down. So, this is the recovery time to make the standby act as primary in a failover.

Here is a typical table that represents application downtime based on availability.

Availability	Downtime per		
	Year	Month	Week
90% (One Nine)	36.5 days	73 hours	16.8 hours
99% (Two Nines)	87.7 hours	7.3 hours	1.68 hours
99.9% (Three Nines)	8.77 hours	43.8 minutes	10.1 minutes
99.99% (Four Nines)	52.56 minutes	4.38minutes	1.01 minutes
99.999% (Five Nines)	5.26 minutes	26.3 seconds	6.05 seconds
99.9999% (Six Nines)	31.5 seconds	2.63 seconds	0.605 seconds

High Availability Solutions in Core PostgreSQL

PostgreSQL offers various HA options that provide a failover mechanism for highly active and critical databases at the time of disaster. It is important that application connections be routed to the standby site for continued data accessibility.

- Warm standby/log shipping

- Hot standby

- Streaming replication

- Cascading replication

Warm Standby/Log Shipping

Continuous archiving can be used to create an HA cluster configuration with one or more standby servers ready to take over operations if the primary server fails. This capability is widely referred to as warm standby or log shipping. This is supported by PostgreSQL at the file level.

The primary and standby server work together to provide this capability with loosely coupled servers. The primary server operates in continuous archiving mode, while each standby server operates in continuous recovery mode, reading the log files from the primary. No changes to the database tables are required to enable this capability, so it offers low administration overhead in comparison with some other replication approaches. This configuration also has minimal performance impact on the primary server.

As the source waits until the log file is full before shipping the log file, there is some delay between the source and the target; the slower the volume of update, the greater the lag between the primary and standby.

The standby server is not available for access in a warm standby configuration, since it is continually in recovery. Recovery performance is sufficiently good that the standby will typically be only moments away

157

from full availability once it has been activated. As a result, we refer to this capability as a warm standby configuration that offers HA. Restoring a server from an archived base backup and roll-forward will take considerably longer, so that technique only really offers a solution for disaster recovery, not HA.

Hot Standby

This feature (available from PostgreSQL 9.0) allows users to create a "hot standby" database instance for read-only queries (SELECTs). Queries execute normally while the standby database continually replays the stream of binary modifications coming from the primary database.

For more information, refer to: `www.postgresql.org/docs/current/static/hot-standby.html`.

Streaming Replication

Streaming Replication (also available from PostgreSQL 9.0) improves the archiving mechanism to make it as up-to-date as possible and to not rely on log file shipping. Standby servers can now connect to the primary and get sent WAL data on-demand as it is generated, rather than waiting for an entire WAL segment to complete.

Streaming replication is asynchronous by default (doesn't wait for confirmation that the changes were applied to a standby server), but as of PostgreSQL 9.1 it can also be configured to be synchronous. The lag on streaming replication is very short, unlike other replication systems, and replicated changes can be as small as a single transaction, depending on network speed, database activity, and hot standby settings. Also, the load on the primary for each standby is minimal, allowing a single primary to support dozens of standbys.

A synchronous replication configuration also supports asynchronous transactions, so that not all changes need to wait for confirmation from the standby server. This means a mix of synchronous and asynchronous can be used in the same system, and can be selected based on how important the data in a particular table is.

To enable streaming replication, the wal_level setting should be set to "archive" or "hot standby."

Refer to the documentation for more details: `www.postgresql.org/docs/current/warm-standby.html#STREAMING-REPLICATION`.

Cascading Replication

PostgreSQL 9.2 provides the ability to stream changes from a standby to other standbys. This can be useful if you have many standbys set up and don't wish to put replication stress on the primary. Refer to the documentation for more details: `www.postgresql.org/docs/current/warm-standby.html#CASCADING-REPLICATION`.

Warm/Hot Standby vs. Streaming Replication

Many people get confused with warm/hot standby and streaming replication and look at them as the same. However, there are some differences.

Warm/Hot Standby

- Both are created with a backup copy of the primary.

- Both work on the basis of WAL apply.

- Both are one WAL behind the primary, so in a worst case, you will lose 16MB of data (i.e., one WAL that is currently being written on the primary).

- The only difference is hot standby can be open for a read purpose but warm standby cannot.

Streaming Replication

- It is quite different than warm/hot standby.

- It works with WAL sender/receiver processes.

- XLOG records for every data modification operation would be sent to standby.

- It is up-to-date with the primary, so in a worst case, you will lose the current transaction that is being executed on the primary.

Simple HA Solution

Let us look at a simple HA solution that can be implemented with one primary and one standby server.

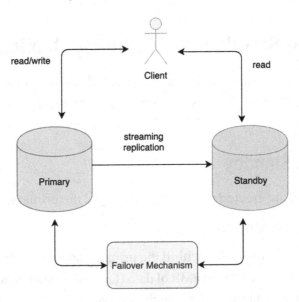

As you see, this solution has one primary and one standby, which are set up through streaming replication.

- Client connects to primary for read/write operation and can connect to standby for read operation

- The failover mechanism here is manual. Either you can create a trigger file on the standby server or promote standby using the "pg_ctl promote" command.

- Once a new primary is available, you would need to update application with new primary details.

This looks like a good solution but not the best. It has a few manual steps, which would increase your downtime in case of failures.

Better HA Solution

Let us look at another solution.

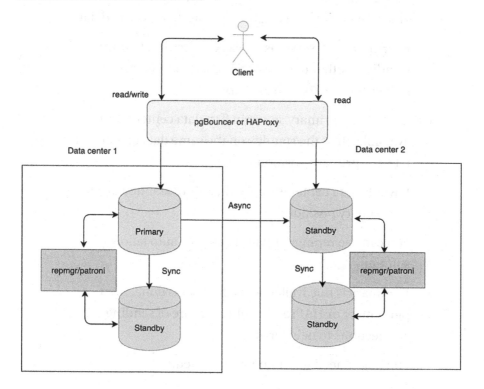

So here:

- Client connects to pgBouncer or HAProxy

- PgBouncer or HAProxy is set up to connect to available server

- Two data centers with one primary and three standby servers

- One primary and one standby in one data center, and another two standbys in another data center

- Replication between primary and standby in same data center is synchronous, as there will not be much delay due to same data center

- Replication between primary and one of the standbys in other data center is asynchronous, as there will be delay

- Fourth standby server is a cascading replica to third standby in other data center. In that way, you can reduce the load on the primary.

- If ONLY the primary server in first data center is not available, then the standby on the same data center will take the primary position

- If whole data center is down, then third standby takes the primary position

- You can use repmgr or patroni as your auto failover solution.

- If primary is not available and failover is done, then pgBouncer or HAProxy would take care of sending connections to new server.

- You might need to set up VIP if needed.

Auto Failover Tools Available

There are many auto failover tools available on the market that you can integrate with PostgreSQL. Here are a few tools:

- repmgr (https://repmgr.org/)

- Patroni (https://github.com/zalando/patroni)

- PAF (PostgreSQL Automatic Failover; https://
  pgstef.github.io/2018/02/07/introduction_to_
  postgresql_automatic_failover.html)

- pg_auto_failover (www.citusdata.com/
  blog/2019/05/30/introducing-pg-auto-failover/)

- pgpool-II (www.pgpool.net/docs/latest/en/html/
  intro-whatis.html)

We are not going to cover all the tools; however, we will show how auto-failover can be done through repmgr. Note that these are only higher level steps to setup.

auto-failover through repmgr

Installation

You can follow this documentation to install repmgr: https://repmgr.
org/docs/4.2/installation.html.

Servers:

```
Primary server - 192.168.0.1
Standby server - 192.168.0.2
```

Make sure keys are exchanged between all these servers.

Setup

On both primary and standby servers, set up a rep_mgr user and a rep_
mgr database on PostgreSQL.

```
psql -c 'CREATE USER REPLICATION rep_gmr';
psql -c 'CREATE DATABASE rep_mgr OWNER rep_mgr';
```

Make sure you create SUPERUSER.

Configuration

Set up the repmgr configuration file on both servers, as they need to be
aware of each other. Location of configuration file is /etc/repmgr.conf.

On primary server:

```
cluster=cls
node=1
node_name=node1
conninfo= 'host=192.168.0.1 user=repmgr dbname=repmgr'
pg_bindir='/usr/pgsql-9.5/bin'
loglevel=DEBUG
reconnect_attempts=1
reconnect_interval=1
logfile='/var/lib/pgsql/repmgr.log'
use_replication_slots=6
service_start_command = 'sudo /bin/systemctl start
postgresql-9.5'
service_stop_command = 'sudo /bin/systemctl stop
postgresql-9.5'
service_restart_command = 'sudo /bin/systemctl restart
postgresql-
9.5'
```

```
service_reload_command = '/usr/pgsql-9.5/bin/pg_ctl -D
/var/lib/pgsql/9.5/data reload'
service_promote_command = '/usr/pgsql-9.5/bin/pg_ctl -D
/var/lib/pgsql/9.5/data promote'
priority=100
failover='automatic'
promote_command='/var/lib/pgsql/standby_promote.sh'
follow_command='/usr/pgsql-9.5/bin/repmgr standby follow -f
/etc/repmgr/9.5/repmgr.conf -W'
```

On the standby server:

```
cluster=cls
node=2
node_name=node2
conninfo= 'host=192.168.0.2 user=repmgr dbname=repmgr'
pg_bindir='/usr/pgsql-9.5/bin'
loglevel=DEBUG
logfile='/var/lib/pgsql/repmgr.log'
use_replication_slots=6
service_start_command = 'sudo /bin/systemctl start
postgresql-9.5'
service_stop_command = 'sudo /bin/systemctl stop
postgresql-9.5'
service_restart_command = 'sudo /bin/systemctl restart
postgresql-
9.5'
service_reload_command = '/usr/pgsql-9.5/bin/pg_ctl -D
/var/lib/pgsql/9.5/data reload'
service_promote_command = '/usr/pgsql-9.5/bin/pg_ctl -D
/var/lib/pgsql/9.5/data promote'
priority=100
```

```
failover='automatic'
master_response_timeout=10
reconnect_attempts=1
reconnect_interval=1
promote_command='repmgr standby promote -f /etc/repmgr.conf
--log-to-file'
follow_command='/usr/pgsql-9.5/bin/repmgr standby follow -f
/etc/repmgr/9.5/repmgr.conf -W'
```

You would need to set up pg_hba.conf entries of the primary server to let the primary server accept replication connections from the standby server.

```
host rep_mgr rep_mgr 192.168.0.2/32 trust
host replication rep_mgr 192.168.0.2/32 trust
host rep_mgr rep_mgr 192.168.0.1/32 trust
```

Please now restart PostgreSQL and the repmgrd daemon.

```
sudo /bin/systemctl start postgresql-9.5
sudo /etc/init.d/repmgrd restart
```

Node Registration

Configuring of both the primary and standby servers is completed, and now we need to verify which server is playing which role.

On primary server:

```
sudo -u postgres repmgr primary register
```

On primary server, you should see:

```
$ psql -U rep_mgr -c 'select node_id, node_name, type, conninfo
from repmgr.nodes' -d rep
```

```
-mgr

node_id |   node_name    |  type   |      conninfo
--------+----------------+---------+------------------
  1     | primary-server | primary | host=192.168.0.1
```

You need to register the standby server now. For that you will need to take a backup, and this is where the backup server comes up.

Let us clone the database on the primary server onto the standby server.

On the standby server:

```
sudo /etc/init.d/postgresql stop
sudo -u postgres repmgr -h '192.168.0.1' -U repmgr -d repmgr -D
/var/lib/pgsql/9.5/data -f /etc/repmgr/9.5/repmgr.conf standby
clone

sudo /bin/systemctl start postgresql-9.5


repmgr -f /etc/repmgr/9.5/repmgr.conf standby register
--verbose
```

On both servers (primary and standby), you see:

```
$ psql -U rep_mgr -c 'select node_id, upstream_node_id, node_
name, type from repmgr.nodes' -d rep_mgr


node_id | upstream_node_id | node_name      |  type   |
--------+------------------+----------------+---------+
    1 |                  | primary-server | primary |
    2 |                1 | standby-server | standby |
```

Test Auto Failover

As the failover option in both (primary and standby) regmgr config files is automatic, if you try to stop the primary, it will promote the standby automatically.

Replication Lag

On PostgreSQL 9.2 and above, this can be found by running:

```
SELECT application_name, pg_xlog_location_diff(sent_location,
flush_location) AS lag
FROM pg_stat_replication
ORDER BY replay_delta ASC, application_name;
```

On PostgreSQL 9.0 and 9.1, the following can be used to calculate the replication lag:

```
DO $$
  DECLARE result int;
BEGIN
  EXECUTE 'SELECT x"' || replace(sent_location,'/',") ||
"'::int - x"' || replace(flush_location,'/',") || "'::int' FROM
pg_stat_replication INTO result;
  RAISE NOTICE 'Replication lag: % bytes', result;
END $$;
```

If there is a large amount of lag, it may be that the network interface being used is contending with other network traffic. This can be caused by other applications running on the same system that use network bandwidth, or that multiple standbys are connected to the primary. If the latter is true, we should recommend cascading replication, where only one standby connects to the primary, and all other standbys connect to the first standby. This, however, is only available on PostgreSQL 9.2 and above.

Common Replication Issues

```
FATAL,58P01,"requested WAL segment 0000000100000B110000000D has
already been removed
```

This can be caused by WAL segment removal from the primary that is required by the standby. This removal is a cleanup process in PostgreSQL. The solution is to ensure proper planning for archive storage. Make sure that archives are getting copied to the standby location, or use a replication slot.

```
FATAL:  could not connect to the primary server: could not
connect to server: No such file or directory
```

This can be caused due to connection loss between the primary and standby. The solution is to set up a script or monitoring tools to check the status of the connection between primary and standby.

```
FATAL:  the database system is starting up
```

If the DB is in recovery, the user should wait till recovery completes. If hot_standby is not enabled, you may see this Fatal error on the standby in case you are using it for read-only queries.

```
FATAL:  terminating connection due to conflict with recovery
```

You can see if there are any long-running queries in the standby. If customers are getting the preceding FATAL error and queries are failing, the DBA needs to check and set the following parameters.

```
hot_standby_feedback
vacuum_diffr_cleanup_age
max_standby_archive_delay
max_standby_stream_delay
```

Why Connection Pooling

Connection pooling is used to cache the database connections and reuse them for future connections. So, it removes the overhead in initializing and closing connections on the database cluster, which can be a huge performance benefit, particularly in environments with frequent and short-lived transactions. It also can provide a queue for connections in excess of max_connections so that incoming connections won't be rejected but instead delayed while they wait for the next available connection from the pool.

There are two connection poolers generally recommended for use with PostgreSQL, although there are many others that will work.

- pgBouncer (`www.pgbouncer.org/`)

- pgpool (`www.pgpool.net/docs/latest/en/html/intro-whatis.html`)

pgBouncer

This is a very lightweight connection pooler that's simple to set up and configure. If connections to a single instance need to be pooled in a simple way, this is the best option. It was originally developed by Skype and was responsible for the entire Skype infrastructure (prior to Microsoft acquisition). Essentially, pgBouncer acts as a transparent database proxy that allows for high-performance reuse of database resources.

From a management perspective, pgBouncer also allows for a dedicate control point for database connectivity. Essentially, a number *n* of pgBouncer servers can be created that can be a funnel for a very large number of application hosts. Since pgBouncer servers can be run as independent entities without any coordination required, there is no issue with scaling this tier very wide. If the pgBouncer tier is scaled, it is recommended the configuration for pgBouncer (just a single pgbouncer. ini file) be controlled by chef or similar to guarantee consistency.

Instructions to set up pgBouncer are here: `www.pgbouncer.org/install.html`.

You can configure using this document: `www.pgbouncer.org/config.html`.

Note, if SSL is added to the infrastructure, pgBouncer is not capable of breaking the SSL connection natively. You can use Stunnel (which is a proxy designed to add TLS encryption functionality to existing clients and server without any changes in the programs), but this sometimes creates problems (`www.pgbouncer.org/faq.html#how-to-use-ssl-connections-with-pgbouncer`).

Issues

There are a few issues that are commonly encountered with Java applications and pgBouncer.

`Unsupported Startup Parameter`

This is an issue caused by the fact that the JDBC driver is always issuing

`set extra_float_digits=...`

To combat this issue, pgBouncer allows you to ignore this parameter at startup and avoid throwing the error. You can set the *ignore_startup_parameters* configuration option in pgbouncer.ini in order to get around this.

pgpool-II

This provides features that pgBouncer doesn't, namely load balancing to allow read-only queries to be distributed among all standbys, and all write queries to continue on to the primary. However, pgpool-II has various caveats and is more complicated to set up and configure than pgBouncer. More about pgpool is here: `www.pgpool.net/docs/latest/en/html/intro-whatis.html`.

Summary

In this chapter, we have talked about the importance of High Availability, and what information we need to build a High Availability solution and the procedures to implement it in PostgreSQL at a core level. We went through a couple of HA solutions. We have mentioned some open source and enterprise tools to implement High Availability. We have also talked about some common issues that we see in the replication point of view. We have covered the importance of a pooler, and available poolers on the market and their implementation.

CHAPTER 8

Basic Errors and Handy Queries

In the last chapter, we talked about why we need High Availability, and what are the different kinds of procedures available to implement High Availability using some open source and enterprise tools available in the market. We also talked about the importance of a connection pooler, available poolers in the market, and how to implement a pooler with PostgreSQL instances. This chapter is basically targeted to the users who just started working with PostgreSQL. In this chapter, we are going to talk about basic errors that we face when we start working with PostgreSQL, and some handy queries that are useful day-to-day for a database administrator.

Basic Errors of PostgreSQL

When you start working with PostgreSQL, you may see a lot of errors while installing, connecting, and querying the databases. Some errors might be very simple to resolve; however, you just need to know the reasons why those errors occur.

Let us categorize the errors based on when they occur:

- Connection errors
- Configuration errors

- Query errors

- Other errors

Connection Errors

This section talks about the errors that we see while connecting to the database. Let us see Errors, and Cause/Resolution for each error in detail.

Error

```
psql -p 5432 -U postgres -d postgres
psql: could not connect to server: No such file or directory
    . Is the server running locally and accepting
      connections on Unix domain socket "/tmp/.s.PGSQL.5432"?
```

Cause/Resolution

This error is caused by unavailability of the socket file in the location where psql is looking. This could be because of reasons like:

1. PostgreSQL is not running.

2. You are using a different port to connect.

    - The first thing you would need to check is server status (using below commands); if the server is not running, start it and try to connect. You can use the pg_ctl utility for checking the status and starting up as follows:

        ```
        $ pg_ctl -D $PGDATA status
        pg_ctl: no server running
        ```

        ```
        $ pg_ctl -D $PGDATA start
        ```

```
waiting for server to start....2019-09-05
22:47:51.551 IST [87688] LOG:  listening on IPv6
address "::1", port 5432
2019-09-05 22:47:51.552 IST [87688] LOG:  listening
on IPv4 address "127.0.0.1", port 5432
2019-09-05 22:47:51.555 IST [87688] LOG:  listening
on Unix socket "/tmp/.s.PGSQL.5432"
2019-09-05 22:47:51.576 IST [87689] LOG:  database
system was shut down at 2019-09-05 22:46:37 IST
2019-09-05 22:47:51.621 IST [87688] LOG:  database
system is ready to accept connections
 done
server started
```

$ **pg_ctl -D $PGDATA status**
```
pg_ctl: server is running (PID: 87688)
/Users//pg_software/11.5/bin/postgres "-D" "/Users//
pg_software/11.5/data"
```

An alternate option to check whether PostgreSQL is running is to check the process status as follows:

$ **ps -ef|grep postgres**
```
1363659639 87690 87688   0 10:47PM ??
0:00.00 postgres: checkpointer
1363659639 87691 87688   0 10:47PM ??
0:00.01 postgres: background writer
1363659639 87692 87688   0 10:47PM ??
0:00.05 postgres: walwriter
1363659639 87693 87688   0 10:47PM ??
0:00.05 postgres: autovacuum launcher
1363659639 87694 87688   0 10:47PM ??
0:00.04 postgres: stats collector
```

```
1363659639 87695 87688    O 10:47PM ??
0:00.05 postgres: logical replication launcher
1363659639 87688       1    O 10:47PM ttys002
0:00.03 /Users//pg_software/11.5/bin/postgres -D /
Users//pg_software/11.5/data
1363659639 87705 27416    O 10:48PM ttys002
0:00.01 grep postgres
       $
```

- If you found that the cluster is running and still not
  able to connect, then check the port number in the
  postgresql.conf file and try to connect using the
  correct port.

```
$ grep -i port $PGDATA/postgresql.conf
port = 5432         # (change requires restart)
```

Error

```
 psql -p 5435 -U postgres -h 192.168.225.185 postgres
psql: could not connect to server: Connection refused
        Is the server running on host "192.168.225.185" and
        accepting TCP/IP connections on port 5432?
```

Cause/Resolution

This error means that there is no service listening on the specified port:
5432. This could be because the PostgreSQL (postmaster) is not listening
for an incoming connection on the port of the network interface. The
default for most of the PostgreSQL distributions is to listen only on the
loopback interface.

1. You would need to look at your "listen_addresses" parameter in the postgresql.conf file; check if you have set this to allow the available network interfaces. A setting to * will cause PostgreSQL to listen on all interfaces.

```
    $ psql -p 5432 -U postgres -d postgres
psql (11.5)
Type "help" for help.

postgres=# show listen_addresses ;
 listen_addresses
------------------
 localhost
(1 row)

postgres=#
```

2. If you found that you set it to allow, then you will have to look at your firewall setting. The port might be blocked by the firewall for that server due to security reasons.

Error

```
 psql -p 5435 -U postgres -h 192.168.225.185 postgres
psql: FATAL:  no pg_hba.conf entry for host "192.168.225.130",
user "postgres", database "postgres", SSL off
```

Cause/Resolution

As the error says, there is no entry in the pg_hba.conf file (which is located at the data directory location) for the HBA (Host Based Authentication) policy for the server. You can add an entry for that host like the following:

- Open pg_hba.conf located in the data directory of the PostgreSQL server.

   ```
   $ vi $PGDATA/pg_hba.conf
   ```

- Add a line like this:

   ```
   host    all                all
   192.168.225.130/32            trust
   ```

Note   Trust is a type of authentication. You will get more info here: www.postgresql.org/docs/current/auth-pg-hba-conf.html.

This policy allows a PostgreSQL client connection from 192.168.225.130.

- Reload the configuration.

   ```
   $ pg_ctl -D $PGDATA reload
   server signaled
   ```

- Now try to connect.

   ```
   $ psql -p 5435 -U postgres -h 192.168.225.185 postgres
   psql (11.5)
   Type "help" for help.

   postgres=#
   ```

As you can see, the new HBA policy allows connection from the client machine.

Configuration Errors

Error

```
$ psql -p 5432 -U postgres -d postgres
psql.bin: FATAL:  sorry, too many clients already
```

Cause/Resolution

This error tells us that total number of client connections reached the max_connections; check the parameter and connections to the cluster from an already connected session:

```
postgres=# show max_connections ;
 max_connections
-----------------
 2
(1 row)

postgres=# select count(*) from pg_stat_activity;
 count
-------
     2
(1 row)
```

To get rid of this, you probably need to increase the parameter or disconnect some "idle" sessions from the application side. Terminating idle connections from the back end could be dangerous, as the application side might get an error. But you may select ad hoc idle connections for termination. You will get idle sessions by using the following query:

```
postgres=# select pid,query,state from pg_stat_activity where
state like 'idle';
  pid  | query | state
-------+-------+-------
 11855 |       | idle
(1 row)

postgres=# select pg_terminate_backend(pid) from pg_stat_
activity where state='idle' and pid <> pg_backend_pid();
 pg_terminate_backend
----------------------
 t
(1 row)

postgres=# select pid,query,state from pg_stat_activity where
state like 'idle';
 pid | query | state
-----+-------+-------
(0 rows)
```

Note   Changing any of the preceding parameters needs a restart of the cluster.

Error

```
    psql -p 5432 -U test postgres
psql.bin: FATAL:  remaining connection slots are reserved for
non-replication superuser connections
```

Cause/Resolution

As the error says, remaining connections are reserved for superusers. So, you would need to increase the max_connections parameter or decrease the superuser_reserved_connections parameter to connect as *normal* user.

Note   Changing any of the max_connections or superuser_ reserved_connections parameter needs a restart of the cluster.

Error

```
ERROR: canceling statement due to statement timeout
```

Cause/Resolution

Use statement_timeout to clean up queries that take too long. Often, you know that you don't have any use for queries running more than x seconds. Maybe your Web front end just refuses to wait for more than 10 seconds for a query to complete and returns some default answer to users if it takes longer, abandoning the query.

In such a case, it is a good idea to set statement_timeout = 15 sec either in postgresql.conf or as a per user or per database setting, so that queries running too long don't consume precious resources and make others' queries fail as well.

The queries terminated by statement timeout show up in the log as follows:

```
hannu=# set statement_timeout = '3 s';
SET
hannu=# select pg_sleep (10);
ERROR:  canceling statement due to statement timeout
```

Query Errors

Error

```
postgres=# select * from test;
ERROR:  relation "test" does not exist
LINE 1: select * from test;
                      ^
```

Cause/Resolution

1. As the first step, ensure that this table really exists.

2. If the table exists, then check whether the table name given is correct or not. You might have created the table with mixed chars (upper/lower). You can get the exact name by using this query:

   ```
   postgres=# select quote_literal(relname) from pg_class
   where upper(relname)='TEST';
    quote_literal
   ---------------
    'TesT'
   (1 row)
   ```

```
postgres=# select * from "TesT";
 t
---
(0 rows)
```

3. Check if you have the table in different schema so
    that you can specify the schema name explicitly
    before the table name OR set the schema name in
    the search_path parameter:

```
postgres=# \d '*'."TesT"

      Table "test.TesT"
 Column |  Type   | Modifiers
--------+---------+-----------
 t      | integer |
```

So, you have the table in "test" schema, then use the
following query or set search_path as shown:

```
postgres=# select * from "test"."TesT";
 t
---
(0 rows)

postgres=# set search_path to "test";
SET
postgres=# select * from "TesT";
 t
---
(0 rows)
```

Error

```
testdb=# drop user bob;
ERROR: role "bob" cannot be dropped because some objects depend
on it
DETAIL: owner of table bobstable
owner of sequence bobstable_id_seq
```

Cause/Resolution

There should not be any object owned by the user when we are trying to drop a user. For dropping such users, there are two methods:

1. Reassign all the objects owned by the user to some other user and then drop the user.

    This is very useful if the employee who left the company has written some procedure/objects that are getting used in an application/process.

    ```
    REASSIGN OWNED BY old_role to new_role;
    DROP USER old_role;
    ```

Note   The reassign command needs to be executed for all the databases under one PG instance.

---

2. First, drop all the objects owned by the user and then drop the user.

    This is useful if the admin doesn't want to keep the users' objects and wants to drop all the objects owned by the user.

    A command that can be used is the following:

    ```
    DROP OWNED BY name [, ...] [ CASCADE | RESTRICT ];
    DROP user username;
    ```

Note   DROP OWNED BY name needs to be executed in all the databases.

Other Errors

Error

```
"LOG: out of file descriptors: Too many open files in system;
release and retry"
```

Cause/Resolution

If you see this error message in a log file, then consider reducing Postgres's max_files_per_process setting.

Error

```
postgres=> copy test from '/tmp/test.txt';
ERROR:  must be superuser to COPY to or from a file
HINT:  Anyone can COPY to stdout or from stdin. psql's \copy
command also works for anyone.
```

Cause/Resolution

As the error says, a normal user can't copy from a file to a table. You can use "\COPY" instead.

```
postgres=> select current_user;
 current_user
--------------
 test
(1 row)

postgres=> \copy test from '/tmp/test.txt';
```

```
postgres=> select * from test;
 t
---
 1
 2
 3
 4
 5
(5 rows)
```

OR

To let a user "test" copy directly from a file, the superuser can write a special wrapper function for "test" user, as follows:

```
create or replace function copy_for_testuser(tablename text,
filepath text)
returns void
security definer
as
$$
 declare
 begin
     execute 'copy ' || tablename || ' from "' || filepath || '"';
 end;
$$ language plpgsql;
```

```
postgres=# \c postgres test
You are now connected to database "postgres" as user "test".
postgres=>
postgres=> select copy_for_testuser('test','/tmp/test.txt');
 copy_for_testuser
-------------------
```

```
(1 row)

postgres=> select * from test;
 t
---
 1
 2
 3
 4
 5
(5 rows)
```

Error

```
ERROR: tablespace "old_tablespace" is not empty
```

Cause/Resolution

As the error says, the tablespace directory should be empty if you are creating a new tablespace. Try to create a new directory or remove the contents from the current directory if they are not useful.

Error

```
postgres=# INSERT INTO cust_view
   postgres-# VALUES (5, 'firstname', 'lastname', 133);
   ERROR:  cannot insert into a view
   HINT:  You need an unconditional ON INSERT DO INSTEAD rule.
```

Cause/Resolution

You can directly insert into a view. So, let us try what the HINT says in the error.

```
CREATE RULE cust_view_insert AS
ON insert TO cust_view
DO INSTEAD
INSERT INTO cust
VALUES (new.customerid, new.firstname, new.lastname, new.age);
```

And now retry our INSERT as follows:

```
postgres=# INSERT INTO cust_view
```

```
postgres-# VALUES (5, 'firstname', 'lastname', 133);
    INSERT 0 1
```

Error

```
postgres=> set log_min_duration_statement to 0;
ERROR:  permission denied to set parameter "log_min_duration_
statement"
```

Cause/Resolution

Several of the parameters controlling logging are reserved to be used only by superusers.

If you want to let some of your developers set logging on, and if you can write a function for them to do just that:

```
create or replace function debugging_info_on()
returns void
security definer
as
```

```
$$ begin
    set client_min_messages to 'DEBUG1';
    set log_min_messages to 'DEBUG1';
    set log_error_verbosity to 'VERBOSE';
    set log_min_duration_statement to 0;
  end;
$$ language plpgsql;

revoke all on function debugging_info_on() from public;

grant execute on function debugging_info_on() to bob;
```

Error

```
postgres=# CREATE OR REPLACE VIEW test_view
  AS SELECT id as title2 FROM test;
  ERROR:  cannot change name of view column "title1" to
  "title2"
```

Cause/Resolution

If you want to change the output definition of a function or a view, then using CREATE OR REPLACE is not sufficient. In that case, you must use DROP and recreate, as follows:

```
postgres=# CREATE OR REPLACE VIEW test_view AS
postgres-#     SELECT id as title1 FROM test;
CREATE VIEW
```

```
postgres=# CREATE OR REPLACE VIEW test_view AS
postgres-#     SELECT id as title2 FROM test;
ERROR:  cannot change name of view column "title1" to "title2"
```

```
postgres=# DROP VIEW test_view;
DROP VIEW

postgres=# CREATE OR REPLACE VIEW test_view AS
postgres-#    SELECT id as title2 FROM test;
CREATE VIEW
```

Error

```
FATAL:  could not create shared memory segment: Invalid
argument
DETAIL:  Failed system call was shmget(key=5440001,
size=4011376640, 03600
```

Cause/Resolution

When PostgreSQL starts, it throws error like the preceding; your
shared memory setting is less than what PostgreSQL is trying to create
(4011376640 bytes in this example). Or your kernel is not configured to
support System-V-style shared memory. As a temporary workaround, you
can try starting the server with a smaller-than-normal number of buffers
(shared_buffers). However, you should reconfigure your kernel-level
shared memory setting. Another reason this error might occur is when you
have multiple PostgreSQL servers running on the same machine. In that
case, all servers' shared memory should not exceed the kernel limit.

Note   Changing shared_buffers needs a restart of the PostgreSQL
instance.

Error

```
In pg_log, "pgstat wait timeout"
```

Cause/Resolution

This warning can happen in several cases.

Case 1 { Huge IO }

When the PostgreSQL autovacuum process is not able to get the required IO to write the statistics to "stats_temp_directory," then we can get this kind of WARNING message. As discussed, the frequent checkpoints are a good indication of high IO. Frequent checkpoints will create further IO, and for analyzing the checkpoints, enabling of log_checkpoints is recommended.

How to log the checkpoints information:

1.   Edit the postgresql.conf file as log_checkpoints = on

2.   Select Pg_Reload_Conf();

Case 2 {Invalid stats_temp_location}

When the PostgreSQL "stats_temp_directory" is in an invalid path, then in this case also we can expect this kind of WARNING message. If you want to change this location to some other place, then you need to follow the below approach.

1.   Edit the postgresql.conf file as stats_temp_
     location='<PATH>'

2.   Select pg_reload_conf();

Case 3 {Invalid Localhost IP}

There might be a chance that we have an invalid Localhost IP. Please check the localhost entries in the "hosts" file and rectify if anything is wrong.

Once we make any changes in this file, we need to restart the PostgreSQL cluster to take its effect on the auto-vacuum worker processes.

Handy Queries of PostgreSQL

This section contains some basic queries that are useful on a daily basis. These queries are categorized into the following:

- Basic queries
- Monitoring queries
- Object privileges queries
- Object level queries

Basic Queries

Let us look into some basic queries.

To Check Version

```
select version();
```

To Check Size of Database

```
SELECT pg_size_pretty(pg_database_size('mydatabasename')) As fulldbsize;
```

To Get All Catalog Tables

```
\dt pg_catalog.*
```

Monitoring Queries

The queries in this section will help you when you are monitoring your database on a daily basis.

Top 10 WRITE Tables

```
select schemaname as "Schema Name", relname as "Table Name",
n_tup_ins+n_tup_upd+n_tup_del as "no.of writes" from
pg_stat_all_tables where schemaname not in ('snapshots','
pg_catalog')
order by n_tup_ins+n_tup_upd+n_tup_del desc limit 10;
```

Top 10 READ Tables

```
SELECT schemaname as "Schema Name", relname as "Table
Name",seq_tup_read+idx_tup_fetch as "no. of reads" FROM
pg_stat_all_tables WHERE (seq_tup_read + idx_tup_fetch) > 0 and
schemaname NOT IN ('snapshots','pg_catalog') ORDER BY
seq_tup_read+idx_tup_fetch desc limit 10;
```

Largest Tables in DB

```
SELECT QUOTE_IDENT(TABLE_SCHEMA)||'.'||QUOTE_IDENT(table_name)
as
table_name,pg_relation_size(QUOTE_IDENT(TABLE_SCHEMA)||
'.'||QUOTE_IDENT(table_name)) as size,
pg_total_relation_size(QUOTE_IDENT(TABLE_SCHEMA)||'.'||
QUOTE_IDENT(table_name)) as total_size,
pg_size_pretty(pg_relation_size(QUOTE_IDENT(TABLE_SCHEMA)||
'.'||QUOTE_IDENT(table_name))) as pretty_relation_size,
pg_size_pretty(pg_total_relation_size(QUOTE_IDENT(TABLE_
SCHEMA)||'.'||QUOTE_IDENT(table_name))) as pretty_total_
relation_size FROM information_schema.tables WHERE QUOTE_
IDENT(TABLE_SCHEMA) NOT IN ('snapshots') ORDER BY size
DESC LIMIT 10;
```

DB Size

```
SELECT datname, pg_database_size(datname),
pg_size_pretty(pg_database_size(datname))
FROM pg_database
ORDER BY 2 DESC;
```

Table Size

```
SELECT schemaname, relname, pg_total_relation_size(schemaname
|| '.' || relname ) ,
pg_size_pretty(pg_total_relation_size(schemaname || '.' ||
relname ))
FROM pg_stat_user_tables
ORDER BY 3 DESC;
```

Index Size

```
SELECT schemaname, relname, indexrelname,
pg_total_relation_size(schemaname || '.' || indexrelname ) ,
pg_size_pretty(pg_total_relation_size(schemaname || '.' ||
indexrelname ))
FROM pg_stat_user_indexes
ORDER BY 1,2,3,4 DESC;
```

Index Utilization

```
SELECT schemaname, relname, indexrelname, idx_scan, idx_tup_fetch,
idx_tup_read
FROM pg_stat_user_indexes
ORDER BY 4 DESC,1,2,3;
```

Tables That Are Being Updated the Most and Looking for VACUUM

```
select relname, /* pg_size_pretty( pg_relation_size( relid ) )
as table_size,
                pg_size_pretty( pg_total_relation_size( relid
                ) ) as table_total_size, */
                n_tup_upd, n_tup_hot_upd, n_live_tup, n_dead_
                tup, last_vacuum::date, last_autovacuum::date,
                last_analyze::date, last_autoanalyze::date
from pg_stat_all_tables
where relid in (select oid from pg_class
                where relnamespace not in (select oid
                from pg_namespace
                        where nspname in ('information_
                        schema', 'pg_catalog','pg_
                        toast', 'edbhc' ) ) )
order by n_tup_upd desc, schemaname, relname;

SELECT schemaname,
        relname,
        now() - last_autovacuum AS "noautovac",
        now() - last_vacuum AS "novac",
        n_tup_upd,
        n_tup_del,
        autovacuum_count,
        last_autovacuum,
        vacuum_count,
        last_vacuum
FROM pg_stat_user_tables
WHERE (now() - last_autovacuum > '7 days'::interval
```

195

```
        AND now() - last_vacuum >'7 days'::interval)
        OR (last_autovacuum IS NULL AND last_vacuum IS NULL )
        AND n_dead_tup > 0
ORDER BY  novac DESC;

SELECT relname, n_live_tup, n_dead_tup, trunc(100*n_dead_tup/
(n_live_tup+1))::float "ratio%",
to_char(last_autovacuum, 'YYYY-MM-DD HH24:MI:SS') as
autovacuum_date,
to_char(last_autoanalyze, 'YYYY-MM-DD HH24:MI:SS') as
autoanalyze_date
FROM pg_stat_all_tables where schemaname not in
('pg_toast','pg_catalog','information_schema')
ORDER BY last_autovacuum;
```

Bloated Index to Run Reindexing (Locking Operation)\ pgrepack (Online Rebuilding)

```
SELECT current_database(), nspname AS schemaname, tblname,
idxname, bs*(relpages)::bigint AS real_size,
  bs*(relpages-est_pages)::bigint AS extra_size,
  100 * (relpages-est_pages)::float / relpages AS extra_ratio,
  fillfactor, bs*(relpages-est_pages_ff) AS bloat_size,
  100 * (relpages-est_pages_ff)::float / relpages AS
  bloat_ratio,
  is_na
  -- , 100-(sub.pst).avg_leaf_density, est_pages, index_tuple_
  hdr_bm, maxalign, pagehdr, nulldatawidth, nulldatahdrwidth,
  sub.reltuples, sub.relpages -- (DEBUG INFO)
FROM (
  SELECT coalesce(1 +
```

```
      ceil(reltuples/floor((bs-pageopqdata-pagehdr)/
      (4+nulldatahdrwidth)::float)), 0 -- ItemIdData size +
      computed avg size of a tuple (nulldatahdrwidth)
    ) AS est_pages,
    coalesce(1 +
      ceil(reltuples/floor((bs-pageopqdata-pagehdr)*fill
      factor/(100*(4+nulldatahdrwidth)::float))), 0
    ) AS est_pages_ff,
    bs, nspname, table_oid, tblname, idxname, relpages,
    fillfactor, is_na
    -- , stattuple.pgstatindex(quote_ident(nspname)||
    '.'||quote_ident(idxname)) AS pst, index_tuple_hdr_bm,
    maxalign, pagehdr, nulldatawidth, nulldatahdrwidth,
    reltuples -- (DEBUG INFO)
FROM (
    SELECT maxalign, bs, nspname, tblname, idxname, reltuples,
    relpages, relam, table_oid, fillfactor,
      ( index_tuple_hdr_bm +
          maxalign - CASE -- Add padding to the index tuple
          header to align on MAXALIGN
            WHEN index_tuple_hdr_bm%maxalign = 0 THEN maxalign
            ELSE index_tuple_hdr_bm%maxalign
          END
        + nulldatawidth + maxalign - CASE -- Add padding to the
        data to align on MAXALIGN
            WHEN nulldatawidth = 0 THEN 0
            WHEN nulldatawidth::integer%maxalign = 0 THEN
            maxalign
            ELSE nulldatawidth::integer%maxalign
          END
```

```
)::numeric AS nulldatahdrwidth, pagehdr, pageopqdata,
is_na
-- , index_tuple_hdr_bm, nulldatawidth -- (DEBUG INFO)
FROM (
  SELECT
    i.nspname, i.tblname, i.idxname, i.reltuples,
    i.relpages, i.relam, a.attrelid AS table_oid,
    current_setting('block_size')::numeric AS bs,
    fillfactor,
    CASE -- MAXALIGN: 4 on 32bits, 8 on 64bits
    (and mingw32 ?)
      WHEN version() ~ 'mingw32' OR version() ~ '64-bit|x86
      _64|ppc64|ia64|amd64' THEN 8
      ELSE 4
    END AS maxalign,
    /* per page header, fixed size: 20 for 7.X, 24 for
    others */
    24 AS pagehdr,
    /* per page btree opaque data */
    16 AS pageopqdata,
    /* per tuple header: add IndexAttributeBitMapData if
    some cols are null-able */
    CASE WHEN max(coalesce(s.null_frac,0)) = 0
      THEN 2 -- IndexTupleData size
      ELSE 2 + (( 32 + 8 - 1 ) / 8) -- IndexTupleData size
      + IndexAttributeBitMapData size ( max num filed per
      index + 8 - 1 /8)
    END AS index_tuple_hdr_bm,
    /* data len: we remove null values save space using it
    fractionnal part from stats */
```

```
    sum( (1-coalesce(s.null_frac, 0)) * coalesce(s.avg_
    width, 1024)) AS nulldatawidth,
    max( CASE WHEN a.atttypid = 'pg_catalog.name'::regtype
    THEN 1 ELSE 0 END ) > 0 AS is_na
  FROM pg_attribute AS a
    JOIN (
      SELECT nspname, tbl.relname AS tblname, idx.relname
      AS idxname, idx.reltuples, idx.relpages, idx.relam,
        indrelid, indexrelid, indkey::smallint[] AS attnum,
        coalesce(substring(
          array_to_string(idx.reloptions, ' ')
          from 'fillfactor=([0-9]+)')::smallint, 90) AS
          fillfactor
      FROM pg_index
        JOIN pg_class idx ON idx.oid=pg_index.indexrelid
        JOIN pg_class tbl ON tbl.oid=pg_index.indrelid
        JOIN pg_namespace ON pg_namespace.oid = idx.
        relnamespace
      WHERE pg_index.indisvalid AND tbl.relkind = 'r' AND
      idx.relpages > 0
    ) AS i ON a.attrelid = i.indexrelid
    JOIN pg_stats AS s ON s.schemaname = i.nspname
      AND ((s.tablename = i.tblname AND s.attname = pg_
      catalog.pg_get_indexdef(a.attrelid, a.attnum, TRUE))
      -- stats from tbl
      OR   (s.tablename = i.idxname AND s.attname =
      a.attname))-- stats from functionnal cols
    JOIN pg_type AS t ON a.atttypid = t.oid
  WHERE a.attnum > 0
  GROUP BY 1, 2, 3, 4, 5, 6, 7, 8, 9
) AS s1
```

```
) AS s2
    JOIN pg_am am ON s2.relam = am.oid WHERE am.amname = 'btree'
) AS sub
-- WHERE NOT is_na
ORDER BY 2,3,4;
```

Bloated Tables to Do Vacuumfull (Locking Operation)\ pgrepack (Online Rebuilding)

```
SELECT current_database(), schemaname, tblname, bs*tblpages AS
real_size,
  (tblpages-est_tblpages)*bs AS extra_size,
  CASE WHEN tblpages - est_tblpages > 0
    THEN 100 * (tblpages - est_tblpages)/tblpages::float
    ELSE 0
  END AS extra_ratio, fillfactor, (tblpages-est_tblpages_ff)*bs
  AS bloat_size,
  CASE WHEN tblpages - est_tblpages_ff > 0
    THEN 100 * (tblpages - est_tblpages_ff)/tblpages::float
    ELSE 0
  END AS bloat_ratio, is_na
  -- , (pst).free_percent + (pst).dead_tuple_percent AS real_
  frag
FROM (
  SELECT ceil( reltuples / ( (bs-page_hdr)/tpl_size ) ) + ceil(
  toasttuples / 4 ) AS est_tblpages,
    ceil( reltuples / ( (bs-page_hdr)*fillfactor/(tpl_size*100)
    ) ) + ceil( toasttuples / 4 ) AS est_tblpages_ff,
    tblpages, fillfactor, bs, tblid, schemaname, tblname,
    heappages, toastpages, is_na
    -- , stattuple.pgstattuple(tblid) AS pst
  FROM (
```

```
SELECT
  ( 4 + tpl_hdr_size + tpl_data_size + (2*ma)
    - CASE WHEN tpl_hdr_size%ma = 0 THEN ma ELSE tpl_hdr_
    size%ma END
    - CASE WHEN ceil(tpl_data_size)::int%ma = 0 THEN ma
    ELSE ceil(tpl_data_size)::int%ma END
  ) AS tpl_size, bs - page_hdr AS size_per_block,
  (heappages + toastpages) AS tblpages, heappages,
  toastpages, reltuples, toasttuples, bs, page_hdr, tblid,
  schemaname, tblname, fillfactor, is_na
FROM (
  SELECT
    tbl.oid AS tblid, ns.nspname AS schemaname, tbl.relname
    AS tblname, tbl.reltuples,
    tbl.relpages AS heappages, coalesce(toast.relpages, 0)
    AS toastpages,
    coalesce(toast.reltuples, 0) AS toasttuples,
    coalesce(substring(
      array_to_string(tbl.reloptions, ' ')
      FROM '%fillfactor=#"__#"%' FOR '#')::smallint, 100)
      AS fillfactor,
    current_setting('block_size')::numeric AS bs,
    CASE WHEN version()~'mingw32' OR version()~'64-
    bit|x86_64|ppc64|ia64|amd64' THEN 8 ELSE 4 END AS ma,
    24 AS page_hdr,
    23 + CASE WHEN MAX(coalesce(null_frac,0)) > 0 THEN ( 7
    + count(*) ) / 8 ELSE 0::int END
      + CASE WHEN tbl.relhasoids THEN 4 ELSE 0 END AS tpl_
      hdr_size,
    sum( (1-coalesce(s.null_frac, 0)) * coalesce(s.avg_
    width, 1024) ) AS tpl_data_size,
```

```
        bool_or(att.atttypid = 'pg_catalog.name'::regtype) AS
        is_na
      FROM pg_attribute AS att
        JOIN pg_class AS tbl ON att.attrelid = tbl.oid
        JOIN pg_namespace AS ns ON ns.oid = tbl.relnamespace
        JOIN pg_stats AS s ON s.schemaname=ns.nspname
          AND s.tablename = tbl.relname AND s.inherited=false
          AND s.attname=att.attname
        LEFT JOIN pg_class AS toast ON tbl.reltoastrelid =
        toast.oid
      WHERE att.attnum > 0 AND NOT att.attisdropped
        AND tbl.relkind = 'r'
      GROUP BY 1,2,3,4,5,6,7,8,9,10, tbl.relhasoids
      ORDER BY 2,3
    ) AS s
  ) AS s2
) AS s3;
```

Real-Time Bloated Tables

```
select relname, n_live_tup, n_dead_tup, (n_dead_tup/(n_dead_
tup+n_live_tup)::float)*100 as "% of bloat", last_autovacuum,
last_autoanalyze from pg_stat_all_tables where
(n_dead_tup+n_live_tup) > 0 and (n_dead_tup/
(n_dead_tup+n_live_tup)::float)*100 > 0;
```

Get name and value from pg_settings

```
select name,setting from pg_settings;
```

Never-Used Indexes

```
WITH table_scans as (
    SELECT relid,
        tables.idx_scan + tables.seq_scan as all_scans,
        ( tables.n_tup_ins + tables.n_tup_upd + tables.n_tup_
        del ) as writes,
                pg_relation_size(relid) as table_size
        FROM pg_stat_user_tables as tables
),
all_writes as (
    SELECT sum(writes) as total_writes
    FROM table_scans
),
indexes as (
    SELECT idx_stat.relid, idx_stat.indexrelid,
        idx_stat.schemaname, idx_stat.relname as tablename,
        idx_stat.indexrelname as indexname,
        idx_stat.idx_scan,
        pg_relation_size(idx_stat.indexrelid) as index_bytes,
        indexdef ~* 'USING btree' AS idx_is_btree
    FROM pg_stat_user_indexes as idx_stat
        JOIN pg_index
            USING (indexrelid)
        JOIN pg_indexes as indexes
            ON idx_stat.schemaname = indexes.schemaname
                AND idx_stat.relname = indexes.tablename
                AND idx_stat.indexrelname = indexes.indexname
    WHERE pg_index.indisunique = FALSE
),
```

```
index_ratios AS (
SELECT schemaname, tablename, indexname,
    idx_scan, all_scans,
    round(( CASE WHEN all_scans = 0 THEN 0.0::NUMERIC
        ELSE idx_scan::NUMERIC/all_scans * 100 END),2) as
        index_scan_pct,
    writes,
    round((CASE WHEN writes = 0 THEN idx_scan::NUMERIC ELSE
    idx_scan::NUMERIC/writes END),2)
        as scans_per_write,
    pg_size_pretty(index_bytes) as index_size,
    pg_size_pretty(table_size) as table_size,
    idx_is_btree, index_bytes
    FROM indexes
    JOIN table_scans
    USING (relid)
),
index_groups AS (
SELECT 'Never Used Indexes' as reason, *, 1 as grp
FROM index_ratios
WHERE
    idx_scan = 0
    and idx_is_btree
UNION ALL
SELECT 'Low Scans, High Writes' as reason, *, 2 as grp
FROM index_ratios
WHERE
    scans_per_write <= 1
    and index_scan_pct < 10
    and idx_scan > 0
    and writes > 100
    and idx_is_btree
```

```
UNION ALL
SELECT 'Seldom Used Large Indexes' as reason, *, 3 as grp
FROM index_ratios
WHERE
    index_scan_pct < 5
    and scans_per_write > 1
    and idx_scan > 0
    and idx_is_btree
    and index_bytes > 100000000
UNION ALL
SELECT 'High-Write Large Non-Btree' as reason, index_ratios.*,
4 as grp
FROM index_ratios, all_writes
WHERE
    ( writes::NUMERIC / ( total_writes + 1 ) ) > 0.02
    AND NOT idx_is_btree
    AND index_bytes > 100000000
ORDER BY grp, index_bytes DESC )
SELECT reason, schemaname, tablename, indexname,
    index_scan_pct, scans_per_write, index_size, table_size
FROM index_groups;
```

Age of DB and Tables

```
SELECT datname, age(datfrozenxid) FROM pg_database;

SELECT c.oid::regclass as table_name,
        greatest(age(c.relfrozenxid),age(t.relfrozenxid)) as age
FROM pg_class c
LEFT JOIN pg_class t ON c.reltoastrelid = t.oid
WHERE c.relkind IN ('r', 'm');
```

Duplicate Indexes

```
SELECT
    indrelid::regclass AS TableName
    ,array_agg(indexrelid::regclass) AS Indexes
FROM pg_index
GROUP BY
    indrelid
    ,indkey
HAVING COUNT(*) > 1;
```

Blocked Queries

```
SELECT blocked_locks.pid      AS blocked_pid,
        blocked_activity.usename  AS blocked_user,
        blocking_locks.pid      AS blocking_pid,
        blocking_activity.usename AS blocking_user,
        blocked_activity.query    AS blocked_statement,
        blocking_activity.query   AS current_statement_in_
        blocking_process
   FROM  pg_catalog.pg_locks          blocked_locks
    JOIN pg_catalog.pg_stat_activity blocked_activity  ON
    blocked_activity.pid = blocked_locks.pid
    JOIN pg_catalog.pg_locks          blocking_locks
        ON blocking_locks.locktype = blocked_locks.locktype
        AND blocking_locks.DATABASE IS NOT DISTINCT FROM
        blocked_locks.DATABASE
        AND blocking_locks.relation IS NOT DISTINCT FROM
        blocked_locks.relation
        AND blocking_locks.page IS NOT DISTINCT FROM blocked_
        locks.page
```

```
          AND blocking_locks.tuple IS NOT DISTINCT FROM blocked_
          locks.tuple
          AND blocking_locks.virtualxid IS NOT DISTINCT FROM
          blocked_locks.virtualxid
          AND blocking_locks.transactionid IS NOT DISTINCT FROM
          blocked_locks.transactionid
          AND blocking_locks.classid IS NOT DISTINCT FROM
          blocked_locks.classid
          AND blocking_locks.objid IS NOT DISTINCT FROM blocked_
          locks.objid
          AND blocking_locks.objsubid IS NOT DISTINCT FROM
          blocked_locks.objsubid
          AND blocking_locks.pid != blocked_locks.pid
      JOIN pg_catalog.pg_stat_activity blocking_activity ON
      blocking_activity.pid = blocking_locks.pid
    WHERE NOT blocked_locks.GRANTED;
Locking session :
SELECT    bl.pid AS blocked_pid,
          a.query AS blocking_statement,
          now ( ) - ka.query_start AS blocking_duration,
          kl.pid AS blocking_pid,
          a.query AS blocked_statement,
          now ( ) - a.query_start AS blocked_duration
    FROM pg_catalog.pg_locks bl
    JOIN pg_catalog.pg_stat_activity a ON bl.pid = a.pid
    JOIN pg_catalog.pg_locks kl
    JOIN pg_catalog.pg_stat_activity ka
          ON kl.pid = ka.pid
          ON bl.transactionid = kl.transactionid
      AND bl.pid != kl.pid
    WHERE NOT bl.granted;
```

```
Blocking query :
SELECT blocked_locks.pid      AS blocked_pid,
        blocked_activity.usename  AS blocked_user,
        blocking_locks.pid      AS blocking_pid,
        blocking_activity.usename AS blocking_user,
        blocked_activity.query    AS blocked_statement,
        blocking_activity.query   AS current_statement_in_
        blocking_process
   FROM  pg_catalog.pg_locks          blocked_locks
    JOIN pg_catalog.pg_stat_activity blocked_activity  ON
    blocked_activity.pid = blocked_locks.pid
    JOIN pg_catalog.pg_locks          blocking_locks
        ON blocking_locks.locktype = blocked_locks.locktype
        AND blocking_locks.DATABASE IS NOT DISTINCT FROM
        blocked_locks.DATABASE
        AND blocking_locks.relation IS NOT DISTINCT FROM
        blocked_locks.relation
        AND blocking_locks.page IS NOT DISTINCT FROM blocked_
        locks.page
        AND blocking_locks.tuple IS NOT DISTINCT FROM blocked_
        locks.tuple
        AND blocking_locks.virtualxid IS NOT DISTINCT FROM
        blocked_locks.virtualxid
        AND blocking_locks.transactionid IS NOT DISTINCT FROM
        blocked_locks.transactionid
        AND blocking_locks.classid IS NOT DISTINCT FROM
        blocked_locks.classid
        AND blocking_locks.objid IS NOT DISTINCT FROM blocked_
        locks.objid
        AND blocking_locks.objsubid IS NOT DISTINCT FROM
        blocked_locks.objsubid
        AND blocking_locks.pid != blocked_locks.pid
```

```
JOIN pg_catalog.pg_stat_activity blocking_activity ON blocking_
activity.pid = blocking_locks.pid    WHERE NOT blocked_locks.
GRANTED;
```

Slow Running Queries on DB from Last 5 Min

```
select now()-query_start as Running_Since,pid, datname,
usename, application_name, client_addr, left(query,60)
from pg_stat_activity where state in ('active','idle in
transaction') and (now() - pg_stat_activity.query_start) >
interval '2 minutes';
```

Delete Duplicate Values in a Table Using CTID (Pseudo Column)

```
DELETE FROM dupes a
WHERE a.ctid <> (SELECT min(b.ctid)
                 FROM    dupes b
                 WHERE   a.key = b.key);
```

Total Number of Transactions Executed in All Databases

```
SELECT sum(xact_commit+xact_rollback) FROM pg_stat_database;
```

Object Privileges Queries

This section provides the queries which you can use to get privileges on object or schema level.

Grant Privileges on All Tables

```
SELECT 'grant select,update,usage on '||c.relname||' to
username;' FROM pg_catalog.pg_class c
    LEFT JOIN pg_catalog.pg_namespace n ON n.oid =
    c.relnamespace
WHERE c.relkind IN ('r',") AND n.nspname='schemaname' AND
pg_catalog.pg_get_userbyid(c.relowner)='username';
```

Check Privileges on Tables

```
SELECT n.nspname as "Schema",
  c.relname as "Name",
  CASE c.relkind WHEN 'r' THEN 'table' WHEN 'v' THEN 'view'
  WHEN 'S' THEN 'sequence' END as "Type",
  pg_catalog.array_to_string(c.relacl, E'\n') AS "Access
  privileges",
  pg_catalog.array_to_string(ARRAY(
    SELECT attname || E':\n  ' || pg_catalog.array_to_
    string(attacl, E'\n  ')
    FROM pg_catalog.pg_attribute a
    WHERE attrelid = c.oid AND NOT attisdropped AND attacl IS
    NOT NULL
  ), E'\n') AS "Column access privileges"
FROM pg_catalog.pg_class c
    LEFT JOIN pg_catalog.pg_namespace n ON n.oid =
    c.relnamespace
WHERE c.relkind IN ('r') AND pg_catalog.pg_get_userbyid
(c.relowner)='username' AND n.nspname='schemaname';
```

Find All Functions with Arguments

```
SELECT n.nspname || '.' || p.proname || '(' || pg_catalog.
oidvectortypes(p.proargtypes) || ')' as FunctionName,usename
as OWNER FROM pg_proc p LEFT JOIN pg_catalog.pg_namespace n
ON n.oid = p.pronamespace, pg_user u WHERE p.prorettype <>
'pg_catalog.cstring'::pg_catalog.regtype AND p.proargtypes[0]
<> 'pg_catalog.cstring'::pg_catalog.regtype AND pg_catalog.
pg_function_is_visible(p.oid) AND p.proowner=u.usesysid AND
n.nspname not in ('pg_catalog','sys');
```

```
select prona.me||'('||pg_get_function_arguments(pg_proc.
oid)||')' as function_arguments,usename,nspname from pg_
proc,pg_user,pg_namespace where  proowner=pg_user.usesysid and
pronamespace=pg_namespace.oid and usename<>nspname and nspname
!~ '^pg_catalog|^information_schema|^sys';
```

Find Privileges of a User on Objects

```
SELECT n.nspname as "Schema",
    c.relname as "Name",
    CASE c.relkind WHEN 'r' THEN 'table' WHEN 'v' THEN 'view'
    WHEN 'S' THEN 'sequence' WHEN 'f' THEN 'foreign table' END
    as "Type",
    pg_catalog.array_to_string(c.relacl, E'\n') AS "Access
    privileges",
    pg_catalog.array_to_string(ARRAY(
      SELECT attname || E':\n  ' || pg_catalog.array_to_
      string(attacl, E'\n  ')
      FROM pg_catalog.pg_attribute a
      WHERE attrelid = c.oid AND NOT attisdropped AND attacl IS
      NOT NULL
    ), E'\n') AS "Column access privileges"
```

```
FROM pg_catalog.pg_class c
    LEFT JOIN pg_catalog.pg_namespace n ON n.oid =
    c.relnamespace
WHERE c.relkind IN ('r', 'v', 'S', 'f')
  AND n.nspname !~ '^pg_' AND pg_catalog.pg_table_
is_visible(c.oid) and pg_catalog.pg_get_userbyid(c.
relowner)='owner'
  ORDER BY 1, 2;
```

Granting Privileges on All Procedures

```
select   'grant execute on procedure
"CBF"."'||proname||'"('||pg_get_function_arguments(oid)||') to
cbf_ctrl_user;' from pg_proc where pronamespace='    <oid of
schema>'    ;
```

Object Level Queries

This section provides the queries which you can use for getting
information at object level.

Get List of All Tables and Their Row Count

```
SELECT
pgClass.relname AS tableName,
pgClass.reltuples AS rowCount
FROM
pg_class pgClass
LEFT JOIN
pg_namespace pgNamespace ON (pgNamespace.oid = pgClass.
relnamespace)
WHERE
```

```
pgNamespace.nspname NOT IN ('pg_catalog', 'information_
schema') AND
pgClass.relkind='r';
```

Check Tables in Each User Defined Schema

```
SELECT n.nspname as "Schema",
  count(c.relname) as "Name"
FROM pg_catalog.pg_class c
    LEFT JOIN pg_catalog.pg_namespace n ON n.oid =
    c.relnamespace
WHERE c.relkind IN ('r',")
    AND n.nspname <> 'pg_catalog'
    AND n.nspname <> 'information_schema'
    AND n.nspname !~ '^pg_toast'
  AND pg_catalog.pg_table_is_visible(c.oid)
 group by n.nspname;
```

Find Parameters Changes for a Table

```
SELECT c.relname, pg_catalog.array_to_string(c.reloptions
|| array(select 'toast.' || x from pg_catalog.unnest(tc.
reloptions) x), ', ')
FROM pg_catalog.pg_class c
  LEFT JOIN pg_catalog.pg_class tc ON (c.reltoastrelid = tc.oid)
WHERE c.relname = 'test'
```

Generate a Script to Change or Rename All Table Names to lower case

```
SELECT 'alter table "'||c.relname||'" rename to '||lower
(c.relname)||';'
FROM pg_catalog.pg_class c
    LEFT JOIN pg_catalog.pg_namespace n ON n.oid =
    c.relnamespace
WHERE c.relkind ='r'
    AND n.nspname='schemaname'
ORDER BY 1;
```

Generate a Script to Change or Rename All Columns of a Table

For Tables

```
SELECT
        'alter table "'||c.relname||'" rename "'||a.attname||'"
        to '||lower(a.attname)||';'
FROM
        pg_class c
        JOIN pg_attribute a ON a.attrelid = c.oid
        JOIN pg_type t ON a.atttypid = t.oid
        LEFT JOIN pg_catalog.pg_constraint r ON c.oid =
        r.conrelid
                AND r.conname = a.attname
WHERE
        c.relnamespace = (select oid from pg_namespace where
        nspname='schemaname')
        AND a.attnum > 0 AND c.relkind in ('r', 'p')
        AND c.relname = 'table_name'
ORDER BY a.attnum
```

For All Tables in a Schema

```
SELECT
        'alter      table "'||c.relname||'" rename "'||a.
        attname||'" to '||lower(a.attname)||';'
FROM
        pg_class c
        JOIN pg_attribute a ON a.attrelid = c.oid
        JOIN pg_type t ON a.atttypid = t.oid
        LEFT JOIN pg_catalog.pg_constraint r ON c.oid =
        r.conrelid
                AND r.conname = a.attname
WHERE
        c.relnamespace = (select oid from pg_namespace where
        nspname='schemaname')
        AND a.attnum > 0
        AND c.relkind in ('r', 'p')

ORDER BY a.attnum
```

Find Primary Keys on Tables of a Schema

```
SELECT c2.relname, i.indisprimary, i.indisunique, i.indisvalid,
pg_catalog.pg_get_indexdef(i.indexrelid, 0, true),
   pg_catalog.pg_get_constraintdef(con.oid, true), contype
FROM pg_catalog.pg_class c, pg_catalog.pg_class c2, pg_catalog.
pg_index i
   LEFT JOIN pg_catalog.pg_constraint con ON (conrelid =
   i.indrelid AND conindid = i.indexrelid AND contype IN ('p'))
WHERE c.relnamespace=(select oid from pg_namespace where
nspname='public') AND c.oid = i.indrelid AND i.indexrelid =
c2.oid
ORDER BY i.indisprimary DESC, i.indisunique DESC, c2.relname;
```

Find Sequences in a Schema

```
SELECT n.nspname as "Schema",
  c.relname as "Name",
  CASE c.relkind WHEN 'r' THEN 'table' WHEN 'v' THEN 'view'
  WHEN 'm' THEN 'materialized view' WHEN 'i' THEN 'index' WHEN
  'S' THEN 'sequence' WHEN 's' THEN 'special' WHEN 'f' THEN
  'foreign table' END as "Type",
  pg_catalog.pg_get_userbyid(c.relowner) as "Owner"
FROM pg_catalog.pg_class c
     LEFT JOIN pg_catalog.pg_namespace n ON n.oid =
     c.relnamespace
WHERE c.relkind IN ('S',")
     AND n.nspname='schemaname'
ORDER BY 1,2;
```

Find the Constraints

```
SELECT r.conname
FROM pg_catalog.pg_constraint r
WHERE r.connamespace = (select oid from pg_namespace where
nspname='public') AND r.contype = 'c'
ORDER BY 1;
```

Find ForeignKeys

```
SELECT conname,
  pg_catalog.pg_get_constraintdef(r.oid, true) as condef
FROM pg_catalog.pg_constraint r
WHERE r.connamespace=(select oid from pg_namespace where
nspname='public') AND r.contype = 'f' ORDER BY 1;
```

Find Parent for ForeignKey

```
SELECT conname, conrelid::regclass, conindid::regclass,
  pg_catalog.pg_get_constraintdef(r.oid, true) as condef
FROM pg_catalog.pg_constraint r
WHERE r.connamespace=(select oid from pg_namespace where
nspname='public') AND r.contype = 'f' ORDER BY 1;
```

Query to Find Sequence OWNED BY

```
select s.relname as "Sequence", n.nspname as "schema",
t.relname as "Owned by table", a.attname as "Owned by column"
from pg_class s
  join pg_depend d on d.objid=s.oid and d.classid='pg_
  class'::regclass and d.refclassid='pg_class'::regclass
  join pg_class t on t.oid=d.refobjid
  join pg_namespace n on n.oid=t.relnamespace
  join pg_attribute a on a.attrelid=t.oid and a.attnum=d.
  refobjsubid
where s.relkind='S'
```

Summary

In this chapter, we have talked about some errors that you see when you start working on PostgreSQL, and their causes and resolution. This will be helpful for the beginners. Also, we have provided some handy queries that you can use on a daily basis. Monitoring queries are useful for a database administrator to check the health of a database.

Index

Printed in the United States
By Bookmasters